STUDIES IN AFRICAN LITERATURE

Writers in Politics

Studies in African Literature

Writers in Politics

ESSAYS

NGŨGĨ WA THIONG'O

LONDON
HEINEMANN
IBADAN · NAIROBI

Heinemann Educational Books Ltd
22 Bedford Square, London WC1B 3HH
PMB 5205, Ibadan · PO Box 45314, Nairobi

EDINBURGH MELBOURNE AUCKLAND
HONG KONG SINGAPORE KUALA LUMPUR
NEW DELHI KINGSTON PORT OF SPAIN

Heinemann Educational Books Inc.
4 Front Street, Exeter, New Hampshire 03833, USA

ISBN 0 435 91751 X (cased)
      0 435 91752 8 (paper)

© Ngugi Wa Thiong'o 1981
First published 1981

Typeset by the Castlefield Press of Northampton
in 11/12pt Journal Roman, and printed in Great Britain
by Spottiswoode Ballantyne Ltd, Colchester and London

Contents

▲▲

To Kim Chi Ha, the great poet of South Korean people and all writers languishing in neo-colonial prisons;

AND

To all those writers in Kenya and elsewhere who have refused to bow to the neo-colonial culture of silence and fear.

Let us not try to be the best or worst of others, but let us make the effort to be the best of ourselves

Marcus Garvey

The profound hypocrisy and inherent barbarism of bourgeois civilization lies unveiled before our eyes, turning from its home, where it assumes respectable forms to the colonies, where it goes naked . . .

When the great social revolution shall have mastered the results of the bourgeois epoch, the markets of the world and the modern powers of production, and subjected them to the common control of the most advanced peoples, then only will human progress cease to resemble that hideous pagan idol, who would not drink the nectar but from the skulls of the slain.

Karl Marx

on The Future Results of British Rule in India

Preface

▲▲▲

These essays were written between 1970 and 1980 and they reflect some of the issues that dominated my mind in the seventies, but which can be summed up in the question: *what's the relevance of literature to life?* The search for relevance immersed me in many ideological debates ranging from questions of culture and education to those of language, literature and politics. This search also saw me move from an intense involvement in the Department of Literature and its many lively debates and activities at the University of Nairobi, to an equally intense involvement in the cultural life of peasants and workers in Limuru. For me, it was a decade of tremendous change: towards the end, I had ceased being a teacher and had become a student at the feet of the Kenyan peasant and worker. The result was my departure from Afro-Saxon literature in order to reconnect myself to the patriotic traditions of a national literature and culture rooted among the people. This change was reflected in my writing of the decade; at the beginning of the seventies I had started *Petals of Blood*, in English, but towards the end of the seventies I had completed *Caitaani Mũtharaba-inĩ*, in Gĩkũyũ language. In the field of theatre, the period saw my collaboration with Mĩcere Gĩthae Mũgo in the writing of *The Trial of Dedan Kĩmathi* in English, to my collaboration with Ngũgĩ wa Mĩriĩ in the scripting of *Ngaahika Ndeenda* in Gĩkũyũ. The period also saw my being hauled from professorial heights at the University of Nairobi to a dungeon in Kamĩtĩ maximum security prison.

The search for relevance was given impetus by three programmes in the Department of Literature: its quest for a relevant literature in Kenyan schools; its popular public lecture series on literature and society; and its struggle for a people-based theatre through its annual project of a Free Travelling Theatre.

Thus, for instance, the essay on literature and society was written for teachers at a literature conference organized at the Department's initiative, at Nairobi School in 1973, on the teaching of literature in Kenyan schools. The paper on 'Writers in Politics' was given in the Department's programme of public lectures. And if the essays are dominated by issues of language and theatre, it is only because the great ideological battle between a pro-imperialist culture and Kenyan national, patriotic culture has been fought out particularly in the theatre.

This ideological battle is, in turn, a reflection of the increasing struggles of the Kenya of the seventies, a period that saw the assassination of J. M. Kariũki and the detention and imprisonment of MPs, workers, writers, students and patriotic intellectuals. The two pieces on J.M. and on his book, *Mau Mau Detainees,* reflect the anxieties raised by the growing right wing political trend in Kenya. It is my hope that the essays should, in a small way, help in the continuing struggle of a national, patriotic culture, reflecting Kenya's interests against the onslaught of a foreign-based culture reflecting imperialist interests.

However, the struggles in Kenya should not be seen in isolation from what is happening in Africa, Asia, Latin America — the whole world. The struggles of the Kenyan people against foreign domination in economics, politics and culture are an integral part of similar struggles in the Third World and elsewhere. I have therefore included some pieces on South Korea and America to show the links that bind us.

I have titled the book, *Writers in Politics,* (because literature cannot escape from the class power structures that shape our everyday life. Here a writer has no choice. Whether or not he is aware of it, his works reflect one or more aspects of the intense economic, political, cultural and ideological struggles in a society. What he can choose is one or the other side in the battle field: the side of the people, or the side of those social forces and classes that try to keep the people down. What he or she cannot do is to remain neutral. Every writer is a writer in politics. The only question is what and whose politics?

NGŨGĨ WA THIONG'O
GĨTOGOOTHI, LIMURU,
KENYA.

PART 1

Literature, Education: The Struggle for a Patriotic National Culture

1 Literature and Society[1]

▲▲

> Ignorant of their country, some people can only relate
> tales of ancient Greece and other foreign lands.
>
> *Mao Tse-Tung*

> If we want to turn Africa into a new Europe, then let us
> leave the destiny of our countries to Europeans. They
> will know how to do it better than the most gifted
> among us.
>
> *Frantz Fanon*

The subject of our three days gathering and discussion is the place and the teaching of African literature in our schools. I hope that the very title will provoke us to anger and protest: how come that it has taken ten whole years after constitutional independence, Uhuru wa Bendera, for us native sons and daughters to meet and to debate for the first time on the subject — the place of our literature in our education system? And why do we find it necessary to qualify this literature with the word 'African', for what else should it be?

A Russian child grows under the influence of his native imaginative literature: a Chinese, a Frenchman, a German or an Englishman first imbibes his national literature before attempting to take in other worlds. That the central taproot of his cultural nourishment should lie deep in his native soil is taken for granted. This ABC of education is followed in most societies because it is demanded by the practice and the experience of living and growing.

Not so in Africa, the West Indies and the colonized world as a whole, despite the crucial role of the twin fields of literature and culture in making a child aware of, and rediscover his environment.

Let me give you three examples:

The other day I found my own son trying to memorize a poem by William Wordsworth. I contained my disappointment and held the book for him while, with a face tortured with the effort, he recited:

> I wander'd lonely as a cloud
> That floats on high o'er vales and hills,
> When all at once I saw a crowd,
> A host, of golden daffodils,
> Beside the lake, beneath the trees,
> Fluttering and dancing in the breeze.

I asked him: What are daffodils? He looked at the illustration in the book: Oh, they are just little fishes in a lake!

Three years ago on a sunny hot afternoon, Okot p'Bitek and I went to a school where one of our former students was teaching. The children hated poetry, she told us: Couldn't we convince them that though poetry was difficult it was a distillation of human wisdom and thought? A gigantic request since we had only one hour between us, but we would do our best. For a start we asked them what poems they had already learnt. Thereupon they told us about a poem of fourteen lines called a sonnet written by one William Shakespeare comparing old age to Winter!

I know of a leading school in Kenya where, on top of Sheridan's *School for Scandal*, Paul Gallico's *The Snow Goose* and other literary vintages in the same vein, (not a single African writer, though they had possibly heard of Chinua Achebe's *Things Fall Apart* and no doubt of Charles Mangua's *Son of Woman* — the latter through the girls' own initiative) they have a text whose title I cannot recall which tells the story of Queen Victoria and how she used to cough and sneeze and eat pudding, and pull her dog's ears and of course anglicize (or is it civilize?) her German husband.

These would be fit cases for jokes and laughter were they not the general practice in our schools. Indeed until a few years ago, the departments of literature (then called English departments) in Nairobi, Dar-es-Salaam and Makerere Universities would only teach British authors from Chaucer through Oliver Goldsmith to Graham Greene. That is how most of us were brought up under the old colonial system administered from the University of London: but is there any reason why our children in this day and age should be brought up on the same impoverished diet administered in the so-called English departments, often headed by some retired biology teachers or retired army majors or men of God, whose main qualifications for the posts are a white skin, long residence in the country, and of course an acquaintance with *The London Book of English Verse*, or *A Penguin Book of English Verse*?

Why was this pattern so in our time? Why does it still persist? Has it all been an accident of content, time, place and persons?

Let us not mince words. The truth is that the content of our syllabi, the approach to and presentation of the literature, the persons and the machinery for determining the choice of texts and their interpretation, were all an integral part of imperialism in its classical colonial phase, and they are today an integral part of the same imperialism but now in its neo-colonial phase. Cultural imperialism, which during colonialism often affected the population and the country unevenly depending on the colonial policies of the marauding powers and the degree of resistance in each country and in different parts of the country, becomes the major agency of control during neo-colonialism.

To support this claim, I must for a few minutes discuss: (1) literature in society, and especially the crucial role played by literature in a people's, any people's, cultural education and in their ordinary daily interaction and contact with other men; (2) how literature was used in the colonization of our people; (3) the role of literature in the anti-colonial national liberation process. Finally, we shall ask ourselves: What is to be done?

Literature results from conscious acts of men in society. At the level of the individual artist, the very act of writing implies a social relationship: one is writing about somebody for somebody. At the collective level, literature, as a product of men's intellectual and imaginative activity embodies, in words and images, the tensions, conflicts, contradictions at the heart of a community's being and process of becoming. It is a reflection on the aesthetic and imaginative planes, of a community's wrestling with its total environment to produce the basic means of life, food, clothing, shelter, and in the process creating and recreating itself in history.

It is important to make that simple and obvious point at the beginning because the general tendency is to see literature as something belonging to a surreal world, or to a metaphysical ethereal plane, something that has nothing to do with man's more mundane, prosaic realm of attempting to clothe, shelter and feed himself.

At the same time literature is more than just a mechanistic reflection of social reality. As part of man's artistic activities, it is in itself part of man's self-realization as a result of his wrestling with nature; it is, if you like, itself a symbol of man's creativity, of man's historical process of being and becoming. It is also an enjoyable end-product of man's artistic labour. But more important, it does shape our attitudes to life, to the daily struggle with nature, the daily struggles within a community, and the daily struggle within our individual souls and selves.

It follows then that because of its social character, literature as a creative process and also as an end is conditioned by historical social forces and pressures: it cannot elect to stand above or to transcend economics, politics, class, race, or what Achebe calls 'the burning issues of the day' because those very burning issues with which it deals take place within an economic, political, class and race context. Again because of its social involvement, because of its thoroughly social character, literature is partisan: literature takes sides, and more so in a class society.[2]

A writer after all comes from a particular class and race and nation. He himself is a product of an actual social process — eating, drinking, learning, loving, hating — and he has developed a class attitude to all those activities, themselves class conditioned. A writer is trying to persuade us, to make us view not only a certain kind of reality, but also from a certain angle of vision often, though perhaps unconsciously, on behalf of a certain class, race, or nation:

> All art aims to evoke; to awaken in the observer, listener or reader emotions and impulses to action or opposition. But the evocation of man's active will requires more than either mere expression of feelings, striking mimesis of reality, or pleasing construction of word, tone or line: it

presupposes forces beyond those of feeling and form which assert themselves simultaneously and in harmony with emotional forces, fundamentally different from them. The artist unfolds these forces in the service either of a ruler — whether despot or monarch — or of a particular community, rank in society or financial class; of a state or church, of an association or party; or as a representative or spokesman of a form of government, a system of conventions and norms: in short, of a more or less rigidly controlled and comprehensive organization.[3]

Seen in this light, the product of a writer's pen both reflects reality and also attempts to persuade us to take a certain attitude to that reality. The persuasion can be a direct appeal on behalf of a writer's open doctrine or it can be an indirect appeal through 'influencing the imagination, feelings and actions of the recipient'[4] in a certain way toward certain goals and a set of values, consciously or unconsciously held by him. A nation's literature which is a sum total of the products of many individuals in that society is then not only a reflection of that people's collective reality, collective experience, but also embodies that community's way of looking at the world and its place in the making of that world. It is partisan on the collective level, because the literature is trying to make us see how that community, class, race, group has defined itself historically and how it defines the world in relationship to itself.

How does this come about? We shall see this clearly if we place literature more centrally in a community's cultural environment and look at its relationship to the totality of a community's activities and experience in the struggle to live.

The basis of all human communities is the soil, land. Without the soil, without land, without nature there is no human community. Quite apart from anything else man is himself of nature. But man detaches himself from nature, observes it and studies its laws with a conscious aim of harnessing them to his service, to his strategy for survival. Unlike the beast that merely adapts itself to its habitation, man through the labour process, acts on the natural environment. In the words of Karl Marx, he 'regulates, controls the material reactions between himself and nature':

He opposes himself to nature as one of her own forces,
setting in motion arms and legs, head and hands, the natural
forces of his body, in order to appropriate nature's production to his own wants. By thus acting on the external
world and changing it, he at the same time changes his own
nature. He develops his slumbering powers and compels
them to act in obedience to his sway.[5]

To harness those laws even more effectively to his sway and
also as a product of the very development of his 'slumbering
powers', man fashions tools, instruments of production, which
together with his labour power (physical, experience, skill etc.,)
constitute his forces of production. He uses tools, technology,
to wrest a living from nature. In the process, he enters into
certain relations, certain arrangements, certain forms of co-
operation with other men suited, of course, to the level of his
knowledge of nature and to the level of his development of his
material forces of production:

In production, men not only act on nature but also on one
another. They produce only by co-operating in a certain
way and mutually exchanging their activities. In order to
produce, they enter into definite connections and relations
with one another and only within these social relations
does their action on nature, does production, take place.[6]

For our own purposes, we can simply say that in the process
of man acting on his natural environment through a combination of his labour-power and technology (tools), and his knowledge of science, he creates a social environment, a social
community. First it is an economic community: i.e. the social
community expresses itself in terms of an economic arrangement,
of certain economic alignments, with different groups standing
in differing positions in the labour process, hence in the production process. The community develops a political structure (the
state, government, administration, etc.), corresponding to the
economic structure, to regulate and enforce those alignments in
the economic structure. In the process, the community expresses
itself in terms of culture. That is, the community develops a
cultural environment in the economic and political processes,
both as a product of these processes and simultaneously with

them as a means of cementing the economic and political structures. Hence the community develops an education system, a legal system, a religious system, a language and literature, forms of dances and songs, in short all the intellectual, moral, ideological forces that give the social relations of production — what we call society — a unique character, a distinctive mark, a certain identity in a particular historical phase.[7] It is the culture that a people have that embodies their values, those aesthetic and moral qualities that they consider basic and important in their contact and interaction with one another, and with the universe. A culture then embodies a community's structure of values, the basis of their world outlook, and how they see themselves and their place in the universe and in relation to other communities. It is the values that a people have that are the basis of their collective and individual image of self, their identity as a people, since culture is an ideological expression of the totality of their activities.

As a people deepen their knowledge of nature, as they develop their instruments of production, and hence change their mode of production (i.e. what, and how, they produce and exchange),[8] so will there occur changes in the political and cultural spheres and hence also in their values and how they look at themselves.[9] Mark you, this is not a mechanical process: how people look at themselves, their values and images of self, will affect their cultural, political and economic structures, their relationship to technology and ultimately their relationship to the soil, land and nature. It is a dialectical process with everything acting on one another to produce the ever changing complexity we call society.

Now a community's knowledge of nature's laws and their skill and experience in the production of tools with which to act on nature do not develop evenly: man's action on nature's space is not always uniform; he does not use nature's laws at the same time, in the same way, in the same degree; the rate of growth and changes in technology are not uniform in time. Equally men's social environment is subject to the same laws of uneven development: man has not always so organized his social environment as to meet the total needs of the members of that community equally with regard to both the quantity and the quality of those needs. The economic structure is at the same time a class structure so that at every level of a community's being, that society is characterized by opposing classes with the dominant class, usually a minority, owning and controlling the means of production, and hence having greater access to the social product, social because it is the product of the combined efforts of men. It is the dominant class which wields political power, and whose interests are mainly served by the state and all the machinery of state power, like the police and the army and the law courts.

Such a class by its command of what is produced, how it is produced, and how that wealth is distributed, has the greater material basis to follow up, develop and control intellectual and ideological forces — education, language, literature, for instance — and hence control the values and the world outlook of the rest of the society. Therefore when we talk about culture, language, literature, ideas, and values of a nation group, a community, we are often talking about the culture and ideas and values of the dominant class in that society. In all economically class-structured societies we would often be more truthful if we talked of two cultures: that of the exploiting class, usually the minority, and that of the exploited class, usually the majority:

> There are two nations in every modern nation . . . there are two national cultures in every national culture. . . . The elements of democratic and socialist culture are present, if only in a rudimentary form, in every national culture, since in every nation there are toiling and exploited masses, whose conditions of life inevitably give rise to the ideology of democracy and socialism. But every nation also possesses a bourgeois culture (and most nations a reactionary and clerical culture as well) in the form not merely of elements but of the dominant culture.[10]

This is clearly seen, for instance, in a feudal society like China, where a definite official literature approved by the ruling dynastic and landed aristocracy co-existed with an underground, unofficial people's written literature. Or it can be seen in a colonial situation where, as we shall see, two antagonistic movements and literary tendencies co-existed. The two were antagonistic because a people's literature, the literature of the exploited classes, no matter how rudimentary or how couched in images and symbols derived from the past, is struggling against the stultifying present and it embodies values and sentiments that look to a future society. Class antagonism at the level of culture and values is only reflecting the reality at the political and economic level where man's development is characterized by class warfare and class political power struggle, which results in different relations of production (i.e. society) with corresponding changes in what constitutes the dominant class and hence the dominant culture, literature and values.

• We can now turn to the nature and practice of this colonial process. In this we shall be talking of a definite, actual historical relationship between a European society characterized by that mode of production (of commodities and for commodity exchange in a market situation) that we call capitalism; and African societies at different stages in the development of their forces of production, at different stages in their action on nature. We shall be talking not only of how Europe underdeveloped Africa,[11] but also how Africa has over the last four centuries continued to develop Europe — to develop European capitalism — through all its main stages with corresponding changes in the forms of relationship between the two continents: from mercantile and *laissez-faire* capitalism where our people were themselves sold as commodities alongside sugar, tobacco and gold (slavery);[12] through the era of industrial monopoly capitalism with the subsequent scramble for and territorial occupation of Africa to control raw materials and create markets (classical colonialism); to the present stage of finance — industrial monopoly capitalism, the era of international trusts, cartels, monopoly combines with aid and the export of finance capital and with the deliberate fostering of a dependent native ruling class in 'independent' states — all to control not only the raw materials and markets, but for continued and thorough exploitation of the labour power of the African peoples (neo-colonialism).[13] Thus for the last four hundred years, Africa has been part and parcel of the growth and development of world capitalism, no matter what the degree of penetration of European capitalism in the interior. Europe has thriven, in the words of C.L.R. James, on the devastation of a continent and the brutal exploitation of millions, with great consequences on the economic, political, cultural and literary spheres.

Thus despite protestations to the contrary from missionaries and other members of the religious, intellectual and spiritual

armies of imperialism, the aim of any colonial mission is to get
at a people's land and what that land produces. This can take
the form of direct occupation, as in the settler colonies of
Kenya, Mozambique, Zimbabwe and South Africa; or at indirect
control, through a colonial government and administration as in
the more commercial colonies of Uganda and West Africa. The
end is the same: to institute an economic structure, and consequently a class system, the colonizing nation can control.

But it is important to keep in mind that although the exploitation of the colonies benefits the colonizing country as a whole,
it is the ruling classes of the colonizing countries that really gain
from colonial and neo-colonial possessions. Dr Norman Bethune,
in an article in *China Today* in 1946, was right to exclaim in
anger:

> Are wars of aggression, wars for the conquest of colonies,
> then just big business? Yes. It would seem so however the
> perpetration of such national crimes seek to hide their
> true purpose under the banner of high sounding distractions
> and ideals. They make wars to capture markets by murder,
> raw materials by rape. They find it cheaper to steal than to
> exchange; easier to butcher than to buy. This is the secret
> of (all bourgeois colonial) wars. Profit. Blood. Money.

But to make economic and political control the more complete, the colonizing power tries to control the cultural environment: education, religion, language, literature, songs,
forms of dances, every form of expression, hoping in this way
to control a people's values and ultimately their world outlook,
their image and definition of self. They would like to have a
slave who not only accepts that he is a slave, but that he is a
slave because he is fated to be nothing else but a slave. Hence
he must love and be grateful to the master for his magnanimity
in enslaving him to a higher, nobler civilization. A slave is not
completely a slave until he accepts that he is a slave. For as
Amilcar Cabral has put it:

> History teaches us that, in certain circumstances, it is quite
> easy for a stranger to impose his rule on a people. But his-
> tory equally teaches us that, whatever the material aspects
> of that rule, it cannot be sustained except by the permanent

and organized repression of the cultural life of the people in question. It can only firmly entrench itself if it physically destroys a significant part of the dominated people.

Indeed, to dominate a nation by force of arms is, above all, to take up arms to destroy or at least, to neutralize and paralyse its culture. For as long as a section of the populace is able to have a cultural life, foreign domination cannot be sure of its perpetuation. At any given moment, depending on internal and external factors which determine the evolution of the society in question, cultural opposition (indestructible) will take on new forms (political, economic, military) with a view to posing a serious challenge to foreign domination. The ideal situation for foreign rule, whether imperialist or not, would be one of these two alternatives: either to practically liquidate the entire population of the dominated country, thus eliminating all possibility of that kind of cultural resistance; or to succeed in imposing itself without adversely affecting the culture of the dominated people, that is to say, harmonizing the economic and political domination of these people with its cultural personality.

The first hypothesis implies the genocide of the indigenous population, and creates a void which takes away from the foreign domination its content and objective: the dominated people. The second hypothesis has not up till now been confirmed by history. Humanity's great store of experience makes it possible to postulate that it has no practical viability: it is impossible to harmonize economic and political domination of a people whatever the degree of its social development, with the preservation of its culture.

With a view to avoiding this alternative — which could be called the dilemma of cultural resistance — colonial imperialist domination has attempted to create theories, which, in fact, are nothing but crude racist formulations and express themselves in practice through a permanent siege of the indigenous population, based on a racist (or democratic) dictatorship.[14]

Some of these crude racist formulations can be seen in the works of leading European thinkers. David Hume, in 1735, was apt to suspect:

The negro is naturally inferior to the whites. There scarcely ever was a civilized nation of that complexion, nor even any individual, eminent either in action or speculation. No ingenious manufactures among them, no arts, no science.[15]

For Thomas Jefferson, a president of the United States of America, a country that had fought against Britain on the basis that all men were created equal, could advance as a suspicion only that:

The blacks, whether originally a distinct race, or made distinct by time and circumstances, are inferior to the whites in the endowments both of body and mind.[16]

As for Hegel, Africa was the unhistorical, undeveloped spirit still involved in conditions of mere nature, and the African was the natural man in his completely wild and untamed state. This opinion was later to be repeated in the 1960s by an eminent historian at Oxford, Trevor-Roper, who in effect argued, to borrow words from Cabral, that 'imperialism made us enter history at the moment when it began its adventure in our countries'.

Anthony Trollope, the English novelist, was sure that Africans had made no approach to the civilization of white creatures, whom he imitated as a monkey did a man:

He is idle, unambitious as to worldly position, sensual, and content with little. . . . He despises himself thoroughly and would probably starve for a month if he would appear as a whiteman for a day.[17]

One could get more quotations of similar quality in racist sickness but these few will do to illustrate how it was that the best minds were employed by the European ruling classes for the cultural genocide of the colonized peoples.

This racism is expressed in the very structure of the English language, probably the most racist of all human languages. It was not only the character of black sambo, but also phrases like black market, black sheep, blackmail, blacklist, black everything, would testify to the value assumptions in that linguistic negative definition of blackness. Those white racist lies were reinforced by religion, Christianity especially, which saw God, Christ, angels, in terms of whiteness, while sin and the devil and satan were black and heaven was depicted as a place where the elect of God would wear white robes of virgin purity, while hell was depicted as a place where the rejects of the white God would burn to charcoal blackness. The South African apartheid system, the most highly developed repressive racist machine of western monopoly capital, is rationalized by biblically derived religious doctrines of predetermination and the notion of a chosen people. So the African Christian, desirous of a place among the band of the saved sang to his maker: 'Wash me Redeemer and I shall be whiter than snow'. If God was slow to respond, there were always hot combs and lipsticks, snowfire and ambi to help the spiritual journey to whiteness and black death.

Cultural imperialism was then part and parcel of the thorough system of economic exploitation and political oppression of the colonized peoples and literature was an integral part of that system of oppression and genocide. It was used in the same way as language and religion. But it was a more subtle weapon because literature works through influencing emotions, the imagination, the consciousness of a people in a certain way; to make the colonized see the world as seen, analyzed, and defined by the artists and the intellectuals of the western ruling classes.

The colonial student was assaulted by European literatures of principally three kinds and in three principal ways.

There was first the good European literature, the product of the best and the most sensitive minds of European culture: Aesychylus, Sophocles, Montaigne, Rabelais, Cervantes, Shakespeare, Goethe, Balzac, Tolstoy, Dostoevsky, Thomas Mann, Ibsen, Yeats, Whitman, Faulkner, to mention a few. These, may I repeat, represent the best and the most refined tradition in European culture and thought. But of necessity their definition of social reality was rooted in their European history, race, culture, and class. When they talked of human conflicts and tensions, when they talked of the human condition and human anguish, they were talking of these tensions and conflicts and anguish as expressed and emerging in the European experience of history. When they talked of man they meant the European man, just as when Americans fought for independence on the basis of the inalienable rights of man, they obviously meant the Anglo-Saxon White Protestant, not the black man.

So the African student was daily confronted with the white image in literature: just as today, he is hit by the same white image in advertisements, on television, on film, in juke-boxes, everywhere. These writers anyway were used for cultural diplomatic export and were used to overawe us who were not known for ingenious manufacture and no arts or sciences. In any case where a writer was good and sensitive, he was used to buy our goodwill and favourable image towards his country — notice the ruthless way in which Shakespeare has been used by the British Council. The interpretation given to this literature by our teachers, white teachers of course, reinforced the image of the European bourgeois with all its narrow-mindedness, bigotry and spiritaul wasteland as 'the universal man'.

The other body of literature was the one that tried to define the colonized world for the European colonizer. This was downright racist literature and often made no effort to hide it. You know the works of people like Rider Haggard (*King Solomon's Mines*); John Buchan (*Prester John*); Rudyard Kipling (the 'Mowgli' stories); Robert Ruark (*Uhuru* and *Something of Value*); Nicholas Monsarrat (*The Tribe that Lost its Head*).

In Nicholas Monsarrat, for instance, Kipling's white man's burden is unashamedly stated as the motive force behind the colonial adventures: where would Africa be without Europe?

> Without Britain, Pharamaul would have been nothing: now at last it was something. It was on the map as a separate country, where before it had been two half-starved warring tribes, eternally at each other's throats, fighting murderously for goats and sand. The process had taken a long time, and lost the lives of many good men; generations of the younger sons of England, pitchforked into this barren waste and told to get on with it. . . . Britain, having come to pacify and discipline, had remained to educate and develop.[18]

In all these European emerges as the hero, the superman, Batman, Tarzan, who can wipe a thousand thick-lipped, big-nosed, curly-haired blacks. The blacks, especially in Rider Haggard, are always of two kinds: the evil ones who are so described that a picture of a devil forms in a reader's mind,[19] and whose one characteristic is an insane hatred of white benefactors out of sheer spite and motiveless envy; or the good ones who are always described in terms of grinning teeth and who always run errands for the white man, tremble in fear when the white man frowns in anger, or show an 'Uncle Tom' face of humility and gratitude for any favour bestowed on them by the European master.[20]

You get a variation of Haggard's two types in the novels of the racist appologist for European settlerism in Kenya — Elspeth Huxley — especially in her two novels, *The Red Strangers* and *A Thing to Love*. Only now her bad evil Africans are those educated in western schools and instead of thanking the Lord for small mercies, actually demand political rights and urge the simple-souled African to violence and sabotage.

Karen Blixen is another writer in the racist tradition. An aristocrat from Denmark she came to Kenya at the beginning of this century and acquired a farm in the now fashionable district of Nairobi still bearing her name. She enjoyed wild animals and naked rugged nature. Later in her book, *Out of Africa*, she was to write:

> When you have caught the rhythm of Africa,
> You find that it is the same in all her music.
> What I learnt from the game of the country was useful
> to me in my dealings with Africans.[21]

She protests her love for natives and animals in the same breath:

> As for me, from my first week in Africa, I had felt a great affection for the natives. It was a strong feeling that embraced all ages and both sexes. The discovery of the dark races was to me a magnificent enlargement of all my world. If a person with an inborn sympathy for animals had come into contact with animals late in life: or if a person with an instinctive taste for woods and forest had entered a forest for the first time at the age of twenty; or if someone with an ear for music had happened to hear music for the first time when he was already grown up; their cases might have been similar to mine.[22]

In all her descriptions of African characters she resorts to animal imagery. The African was really part of the woods and animals,

part of Hegel's unconscious nature. She gives medicine to
Kamante and after he is cured he becomes her very good cook.

> Kamante could have no idea as to how a dish of ours
> ought to taste, and he was, in spite of his conversion, and
> his connexion with civilization, at heart an arrant Kikuyu,
> rooted in the traditions of his tribe and his faith in them,
> as in the only way of living worthy of a human being. He
> did at times taste the food that he cooked, but then with a
> distrustful face, like a witch who takes a sip out of her
> cauldron. *He stuck to the maizecobs of his fathers*. Here
> even his intelligence sometimes failed him, and he came
> and offered me a Kikuyu delicacy a roasted sweet potato
> or a lump of sheep's fat — *as even a civilized dog, that has
> lived for a long time with people, will place a bone on the
> floor before you, as a present.*[23] (italics mine)

When she goes back to Denmark, her African characters keep
on visiting her in her dreams — but in the form of animals.

> It was then that my old companions began to put in an
> appearance in my dreams at night, and by such behaviour
> managed to deeply upset and trouble me. For till then no
> living people had ever found their way into those dreams.
> They came in disguise, it is true, and as in a mirror darkly,
> so that I would at times meet Kamante in the shape of a
> dwarf-elephant or a bat, Farah as a watchful leopard snarl-
> ing lowly round the house, and Sirunga as a small jackal,
> yapping — such as the natives tell you that jackals will do
> in times of disaster with one forepaw behind his ear. But
> the disguise did not deceive me, I recognised each of them
> every time and in the mornings I knew that we had been
> together, for a short meeting on a forest path or for a
> journey. So I could no longer feel sure that they did still
> actually exist, or indeed that they had ever actually existed,
> outside of my dreams.[24]

Her cosmos is hierarchically ordered with God at the top
followed by the white aristocracy, ordinary whites, domestic
animals, wild animals who are all in 'direct contact' with God.
Africans don't figure anywhere in this cosmic picture except as

parts of wood and stones, different only because occasionally they exhibit impulses towards animals.

Karen Blixen was once proposed by Hemingway for the Nobel prize in Literature.

I quoted from Blixen liberally because she was no ordinary drunken soldier or an uncouth frustrated missionary spinster come to Africa to fulfil herself in lording it over schoolgirls and terrorizing timid African teachers but a refined lady of some discrimination and learning. She belongs to the same tradition of great racists like Hume, Trollope, Hegel, Trevor-Roper and all other arch-priests of privilege, racism and class snobbery.

The last group of writers I want to mention are those who set out to sympathetically treat the African world either to appeal to the European liberal conscience or simply to inter-pret Africa for the Africans. But even among these, the African image is still in negative terms. For Joseph Conrad, the African characters in *Heart of Darkness* are part of that primitive savagery that lay below the skin of every civilized being. He was telling his fellow Europeans: You go to Africa to civilize, to enlighten a heathen people; scratch that thin veneer of civilization and you will find the savagery of Africa in you too. For Joyce Cary, the positive creative African in *Mister Johnson* is a clowning idiot whose desire and final fulfilment is having to be shot dead by an Englishman whom we are led to believe loves him well. We all love our horses and dogs and cats and we often shoot them to put them out of pain. So much for *Mister Johnson* and Master Joyce Cary. For William Blake, the little black boy, cries thus:

> My mother bore me in the southern wild,
> And I am black, but O, my soul is white
> White as an angel is the English child,
> But I am black as if bereaved of light.[25]

He longs for the day he will die and be freed from the burden of his skin colour, then he and the white boy will 'lean in joy upon our Father's knee':

> And then I'll stand and stroke his silver hair,
> And be like him, and he will then love me.[26]

This is the white liberal's dream of a day when black and white can love one another without going through the agony of violent reckoning. Liberalism has always been the sugary ideology of imperialism: it fosters the illusion in the exploited of the possibilities of peaceful settlement and painless escape from imperialist violence which anyway is not called violence but law and order. Liberalism blurs all antagonistic class contradictions, all the contradictions between imperialist domination and the struggle for national liberation, seeing in the revolutionary violence of the former, the degradation of humanity:

> Liberalism rejects ideological struggle and stands for unprincipled peace, thus giving rise to a decadent, philistine, attitude and bringing about political degeneration in certain units and individuals (among the oppressed) . . . and objectively has the effect of helping the enemy [i.e. imperialism].[27]

And nowhere is liberalism so clearly manifested as in imaginative literature.

You can see this more clearly in Alan Paton's *Cry the Beloved Country*. Here the good African exemplifies the Christian virtue of spineless humility and a longing to be loved by the enemy which of course is an element of self-hatred and negative self-definition. Looking around him Alan Paton sees the physical, religious and intellectual violence inflicted on the African by a colonial system that would more than meet with Hitler's full approval. He can see, and knows it anyway, that it is the white fascist minority that has brought the barracks, the prisons, the police station, the black maria, the gun — all the instruments of state violence to keep the African in actual hell — while the ruling classes in Europe (the Anglo-American monopoly combines, the Oppenheimer empire, etc.) reap their thirty pieces of silver and cry shame to Nixonian Hitler. Alan Paton knows, with Frantz Fanon, that decolonization is a violent process. One day the black South African workers, the *tsotsis*, the *Lumpenproletariat*, the peasants, will meet this reactionary violence with revolutionary regenerative violence. This is the possibility that scares Alan Paton. So he writes a book, a novel depicting an African who has been completely emasculated by the Christian church, a man who not only eschews the mildest form of violence but is seen as being incapable of anger even, as a positive hero.

To show you the sickness, the pious pusillanimous dream and flabby hopes in the novel, I have chosen a passage depicting the final meeting between Jarvis and Stephen Kumalo up on Martin Luther King's mountain of wishful dreams. Here Blake's white boy reappears with the bright eyes of tomorrow's saving angel, and the black boy regains hope and faith and cries in gratitude to the white man for donating a pittance to the church and for speaking kindly to him:

They stayed there in silence till Jarvis said, Umfundisi, I must go. But he did not go. Instead he said, Where are you going at this hour?
Kumalo was embarrassed, and the words fell about on his tongue, but he answered, I am going into the mountain. Because Jarvis made no answer he sought for words to explain it, but before he had spoken a word, the other had already spoken. I understand you, he said, I understand completely.

And because he spoke with compassion, the old man wept, and Jarvis sat embarrassed on his horse. Indeed he might have come down from it, but such a thing is not lightly done. But he stretched his hand over the darkening valley, and he said, One thing is about to be finished, but here is something that is only begun. And while I live it will continue. Umfundisi, go well.
Umnumzana!
Yes.
Do not go before I have thanked you. For the young man, and the milk. And now for the church.
I have seen a man, said Jarvis with a kind of grim gaiety, who was in darkness till you found him. If that is what you do, I give it willingly.
Perhaps it was something deep that was here, or perhaps the darkness gives courage, but Kumalo said, *Truly, of all the white men that I have ever known . . .*
I am no saintly man, said Jarvis fiercely.
Of that I cannot speak, but God put His hands on you.
And Jarvis said, That may be, that may be. He turned suddenly to Kumalo. Go well, umfundisi. Throughout this night, stay well.

> *And Kumalo cried after him, Go well, go well.*[28] (italics
> mine)

Reading Alan Paton, and the works of other liberal writers,
we should ask ourselves: Why is it that the church is always
preaching humility and forgiveness and non-violence to the
oppressed? Why do the liberals preach gratitude, humility, kind-
ness, forgiveness and meekness to the oppressed classes? Why is
it that the church does not concentrate its preaching and efforts
of conversion on the very classes and races that have brutalized
others, manacled others, robbed others?

The aim is obvious: it is to weaken the resistance of the
oppressed classes and here imaginative literature comes in as
a useful medium of mental conditioning, making the oppressed
believe that the root cause of their problem, and hence the
solution, lies deep in their spiritual condition, in their sinful souls.

This then is the kind of literature, the kind of literary fare
being ladled to our children, even today: what greater violence
to our sense of being? This kind of literature was aptly described
by Edward Blyden in 1883 when he wrote:

> All our traditions and experiences are connected with a
> foreign race. We have no poetry or philosophy but that of
> our taskmasters. The songs that live in our ears and are
> often on our lips are the songs which we heard sung by
> those who shouted while we groaned and lamented. They
> sang of their history, which was the history of our degrada-
> tion. They recited their triumphs, which contained the
> records of our humiliation. To our great misfortune, we
> learned their prejudices and their passions, and thought
> we had their aspirations and their power.[29]

He summed the whole effect of cultural imperialism on the
psyche of the African child in the following words:

> In all English-speaking countries the mind of the intelligent
> Negro child revolts against the descriptions given in ele-
> mentary books — geographies, travels, histories — of the
> Negro; but though he experiences an instinctive revulsion
> from the caricatures and misrepresentations, he is obliged
> to continue, as he grows in years, to study such pernicious

teachings. After leaving school he finds the same things in
newspapers, in reviews, in novels, in *quasi* scientific works,
and after a while — *sape cadendo* — they begin to seem to
him the proper things to say and to tell about his race, and
he accepts what, at first, his fresh and unbiased feelings
naturally and indignantly repelled. Such is the effect of
repetition.

Having embraced, or at least assented, to these errors
and falsehoods about himself, he concludes that his only
hope of rising in the scale of respectable manhood is to
strive after whatever is most unlike himself and most alien
to his peculiar tastes.[30]

Under classical colonialism, the effect of that kind of literature was to produce an African permanently injured by a feeling
of inadequacy, a person who would look up with reverent awe
to the achievements of Europe; a person, who like Kumalo in
Cry the Beloved Country has no faith either in himself, or in the
capacity of his people for total liberation; a person who cries
with gratitude at the Blixenian—Jarvis type of love and kind
words. Above all, this literature, and the whole approach to
literary and cultural education, inculcated in some of our people
the values of the European ruling class and made our own rising
middle class take on those values for a universal norm. This has
been responsible for the mental structure of dependence so
evident in ourselves, so evident in our rising bourgeoisie: else
why do we still retain advisers of dubious quality and qualifications in all our spheres of national life? Why do we still retain
foreign headmasters, foreign teachers of literature, language,
history, religion, in our schools under the cloak of that dirty
euphemism — experience? What use is experience in an old
structure of values we want to get rid of? Experience anyway
comes out of practice, participation and challenge.

But more important, this kind of education typified by
that approach to literature, was part of a calculated policy to
nurture a dependent native middle class sharing the values of
exploitation, to take positions of influence after constitutional
independence.

This class born and thriving under colonialism but whose
growth to its full height and status as the national middleman
of international industrial and finance monopoly capitalism was

blunted by the racism inherent in direct colonial control, now becomes the main beneficiary of constitutional or flag independence. Its interests therefore lie in maintaining in fact the structure of capitalism and their alliance with the imperialist bourgeoisie. Faithfully obeying the laws of capitalist accumulation, it becomes at least in the initial stages of its flowering, the greatest ally of international finance capital and the international ruling class. Neo-colonialism then means the continued economic exploitation of Africa's total resources and of Africa's labour power by international monopoly capitalism through continued creation and encouragement of subservient weak capitalistic economic structures, captained or overseered by a native ruling class. In the political sphere, this class will often make defence pacts and arms agreements with the former colonial masters as a guarantee of its continued claim to political power. A political characteristic of this class is its discomfiture with the masses. The masses (peasants, workers) are not to be trusted and ethnic divisions are now actively encouraged and perpetuated.

· The discomfiture with the masses so evident among the ruling political circles is present in most African novels even at their most radical and critical. The crowds emerge as gullible, easily fooled, praising now this leader then that leader in return for a drink of beer and five cents. They are often depicted as watchers and applauders of *Andu Agima*. The masses are seen as having no minds of their own. African writers themselves being part of the petty intellectual army of this native ruling class (note that most of them are products of colonial universities) have never really accepted the possibility of their becoming true literary guerrillas of the masses in their quest and struggle for total liberation. In African literature, we have very few positive heroes from among the working people, positive heroes who would embody the spirit of struggle and resistance against exploitation and naked robbery by the national bourgeoisie and its global allied classes.

In the realm of culture and values then, this class becomes the main agency for cultural imperialism. So that apart from continuing to import the personnel to run our humanities departments (often through cultural-technical aid agreements); apart from continuing to import foreign literature into our schools and universities and making it the corner-stone of our studies, we are encouraged to produce and are applauded for producing the kind of literature that perpetuates the same decadent western bourgeois values and class world outlook. If you think that I am exaggerating about this encouragement, you have only to look around you and see the mad rush of European critics who only a few years ago, before independence, were so disparaging about African literature and African writers. Now they are the new interpreters, interpreting African literature for the African. You can't win, can you?

But sadder still is when you get our own African critics continuing the same aged approach to literature, the same mouthing of phrases about the anguish of the human condition, universal values that transcend race, class, economics, politics and other social activities of ordinary living.

It is important that we understand that cultural imperialism in its era of neo-colonialism is a more dangerous cancer because it takes new subtle forms and can hide even under the cloak of militant African nationalism, the cry for dead authentic cultural symbolism and other native racist self assertive banners. Suddenly under neo-colonialism it is the African who is building churches in every village under Harambee self-help schemes; who is rushing for the latest literary trash from America or failing that, Africanizing the same thrills and escapism by giving them local colour; who will tell you about the latest fashions in clothes, songs and dances from New York; who will import hot combs, ambi, and other skin lightening creams; who will be horrified at the idea of planning a man-made social environment but will be ecstatic about family planning, i.e. planning human beings; who will defend with the greatest possible fervour the decaying values of the Western ruling circles.

It is the African ruling classes, once described by Fanon as having a permanent wish for identification with the bourgeois representatives of the mother country, who under neo-colonialism become the missionary agency for the continuation of cultural imperialism as part and parcel of imperialism's economic and political encirclement of the world.

Having painted a picture full of gloom and pessimism, it might be asked is there nothing to be done? What must now be done? I hope we shall debate that question in the next two days and after. But we can learn a lesson from the anti-colonial process, from the whole historical struggle for national liberation. This struggle is simply a dialectical negation of the colonial process outlined above. For a colonized people, Fanon has written, the most essential value, because the most concrete, is first and foremost the land. People want to control their soil, their land, the fruits of their labour-power acting on nature; to control their history made by their collective struggle with their natural and social environment. Cabral has said that since for both colonialism and neo-colonialism:

> The essential characteristic of imperialist domination remains the same: the negation of the historical process of the dominated people by means of violent usurpation of the freedom of development of the national productive forces. . . . We can state that the national liberation is the phenomenon in which a given socio-economic whole rejects the negation of the historical process. In other words, the national liberation of a people is the regaining of the historical personality of that people, its return to history through destruction of the imperialist domination to which it was subjected. . . . National liberation exists only when the national productive forces have been completely freed from every kind of foreign domination.[31]

This is why the anti-colonial process is primarily an economic and political struggle and in essence is incompatible with the economic structure of capitalism.

Under colonialism, this economic and political struggle is often waged under the petty-bourgeois banner of racial nationalism. It is 'we' black people against 'them' whites; Africans versus Europeans. This is only natural since under colonialism, exploitation and privilege masquerade or take the form of an ironrace-caste structure. But under neo-colonialism, the political and economic struggle assumes its true class character despite any and every attempt at ethnic mystification. It is now African workers and the peasant masses, together with progressive intellectuals, patriotic elements, students and their class allies from other parts of the world, pitted against the native ruling class and its international imperialist class allies.

But the anti-colonial and anti-imperialist (i.e. anti-neo-colonial struggle) is also waged at the level of culture and values. In other words, for the anti-colonial, anti-imperialist political and economic struggle to be complete, it must also be a cultural struggle since the aim is to restore the African personality to its true human creative potentialities in history, so as to enhance the quality of life and of life-based values.

Indeed most national liberation movements start by rejecting the culture of the colonizer, by repudiating the religion of the oppressing nation and class and the entire education system of the colonizer. People create their own songs, poems, dances, literature, which embody a structure of values dialectically opposed to those of the ruling class of the oppressing race and nation. Often they will take the songs of the colonizer and give them an entirely different meaning, interpretation and emphasis.

We shall go no further than Mau Mau. Mau Mau was Kenya's national liberation movement that opted for the armed struggle as the highest form of political and economic struggle. On top of demanding back the land and power, they rejected the culture of the oppressor and created a popular oral literature embodying anti-exploitation values. They took Christian songs; they took even the Bible and gave these meanings and values in harmony with the aspirations of their struggle. Christians had often sung about heaven and angels, and a spiritual journey in a spiritual intangible universe where metaphysical disembodied evil and good were locked in perpetual spiritual warfare. Christians sang:

Aanake ũkĩraai	Young men arise
Mũũgwĩtwo nĩ Jesu	Jesus calls you to
Muoe matimũ na Ngo	Take up spears and shields and to
Mũte guoya wanyu	Throw away your fears.
Ukĩrĩ wake guoya	For what's the point of fear?
Thĩĩ na ũcaamba;	Go ye with bravery;
Mũtwarĩĩtwo nĩ Jesũ	Led by Jesus
No mũkaahootana.[32]	You'll be victorious.

The Mau Mau revolutionaries took up the same song and tune and turned it into a song of actual political, visible material freedom and struggle for land. The battle was no longer in heaven but here on earth, in Kenya. So they sang:

Aanake ũkĩraai	Young men arise
Mũũgwĩtwo nĩ Mbiũ	Mbiũ calls you to
Muoe Matimũ na ngo	Take up spears and shields

Na mũtigaikare.	And don't delay.
Ũmaai na Ihenya	Get out quickly
Ũkaai Mũteithanie	Come help one another
Ageni nĩ Nyakeerũ	The white people are foreigners
Na nĩ njaamba nene.[33]	And they are very strong
	(i.e. well-armed).

The song goes on to ask the patriots to eschew drinking; they should only take up things made by Kenyan people, for with such things they would never be defeated. It further calls on them to cast away fear and cowardice (*ũkĩrĩ wakĩ guoya*) and step up political agitation among the masses. With justice being on their side they would truly emerge victorious from their anti-imperialist struggle.

Mbaara ĩrĩa tũraarũa	The war we are fighting
Nĩ ya ithaka ciitũ	It is for our lands
Na kũrĩ andũ amwe aitũ	But there are some of our people
Maroiga ti ciitũ	Who say the lands are not ours.
Kaĩ o mataroona	Can't they see
Thĩĩna ũrĩa tũraaheeo?	The oppression inflicted on us?
Tũraathĩĩnĩrio ithaka	We are being tortured for lands
Twaheirwo nĩ Ngai	We were given by God.

There were other songs. Christians sang:

Maikarite Thĩ ũtukũ	They sat down by night
Arĩĩthi a Mburi	Shepherds of sheep
Mũrekio wa Ngai nĩ ookire	The angel of the Lord came
Na ũtheri mũnene.[34]	With bright light.

The Mau Mau sang:

Maikarĩĩte Kaloleni	They sat at Kaloleni
Arĩĩthi a KAU	Shepherds of KAU
Magĩthoondeka meeciiria	Thinking out plans
Ma gũthĩĩ Rũraaya.[35]	Of how to go to England (i.e. to send a political delegation to Europe).

They go on to sing about the one who is born today, a leader of the people in their struggle for political rights, social justice and for the recovery of the stolen lands.

Christians sang of the happy day when 'I first became a convert and Jesus cleansed me'. The Mau Mau sang of the 'happy day, when they first sent their spokesman to UNO (United National Organization). There were many others in a similar vein. It was as if the people of Kenya did to the Christian universe and spiritual idealism what Marx did to Hegel's dialectics: made them stand firmly on the ground, our earth, instead of standing on their head. The aim, in other words, is to change a people's world outlook, it is to seize back the right and the initiative to define oneself.

A written literature also develops alongside people's oral fighting literature again as part of the cultural struggle and cultural assertion. In the case of Africa, the very act of writing was itself a testimony of the creative capacity of the African and the first tottering but still important steps by the 'educated' elite towards self-definition and the acceptance of the environment from which they had been alienated by western, Eurocentric imperialist education. But the literature produced, because of its critical realism, also reflected the reality of the African struggle against colonial domination.

Chinua Achebe is a case in point. His novels taken as a whole beautifully delineate the origins, growth and development of a neo-colonial native ruling class. This class has roots in the early Christian converts, the early *asomi* who learnt to read and write; the court messengers; the policemen; the road overseers, in *Things Fall Apart* and *Arrow of God*. This class later becomes the backbone of the business and civil service 'been to's' in *No Longer at Ease*. In *A Man of the People*, the class inherits power and begins to fulfil its historical mission of a messenger class, in the process looting the people. Where the individual messenger was bribed by individual families in *Things Fall Apart*; where the same individual messenger played one clan against another to confuse them about his messenger role and cloud it with nepotism and hence eat the bribe in peace in *Things Fall Apart* and *Arrow of God*, the same class now extorts bribes from the whole country in *A Man of the People* and plays one ethnic community against others on a national scale, again to mystify its true role and character as a messenger class. In *Girls at War*, the class involves the whole country in bloodshed in its intra-class warfare for a share of the cake, the left-overs, given to it by the master.

Such a literature, again at its critical best and most committed, defines a people not in terms of always being acted on but in terms of actors. Okonkwo and Ezeulu as representatives of the people and people's spirit of resistance make their own history. Okonkwo commits suicide rather than submit and live in a world where he is denied the right to make his own history through his control and development of the productive forces. His act of killing an imperialist messenger is as symbolic as it is prophetic. It is the new messenger class, the new errand boys of international monopoly capitalism that make total liberation difficult, for on the surface they do look like one of Okwonkwo's own people.

I believe that we as teachers of literature can help in this collective struggle to seize back our creative initiative in history. For this it is essential that we grasp the true function and role of literature in our society. We can help principally in three ways:

(1) In all our schools, teacher training colleges and community centres we must insist on the primacy and centrality of African literature and the literature of African people in the West Indies and America. Central to this is the oral literature of our people, including their contemporary compositions.

(2) Where we import literature from outside, it should be relevant to our situation. It should be the literature that treats of historical situations, historical struggles, similar to our own. It should be the kind of literature that rejects oppressive social-economic systems, that rejects all those forces that dwarf the creative development of man. In this case anti-imperialist literatures from Asia and Latin America and literature from socialist countries are very important. But anti-imperialist, anti-bourgeois literature and the pro-people literature of struggle from writers in imperialist countries can add a considerable contribution to our own struggles for a better world.

(3) While not rejecting the critical demands of the more formal elements and needs of any art, we must subject literature whether oral, African or from other lands to a most rigorous criticism from the point of view of the struggling masses. We must detect what is positive, revolutionary, humanistic in a

work of art, support it, strengthen it; and reject what is negative and anti-humanistic in the same or other works.

All this is not easy for it calls upon us to re-examine ourselves, our values, our own world outlook, our own assumptions and prejudices. Above all, it demands of us to re-examine our own stand and attitude to the struggle that still goes on in our continent: the struggle of our people against economic, political, and cultural imperialism of western European and Japanese capitalism, whose most ugly deformation is seen in South Africa, Rhodesia, Angola and Mozambique. It demands of us to adopt a scientific materialistic world outlook on nature, human society and human thought, and assume the standpoint of the most progressive and revolutionary classes (i.e. workers and peasants) in our society, for they are at the forefront in the struggle against imperialism and foreign domination, indeed against the suffocating alliance between the imperialist bourgeoisie and the local pro-foreigner *comprador* class.

In his last days in Conakry, Kwame Nkrumah wrote that the spectre of Black Power was haunting the world. Black Power here does not mean a glorification of an ossified past. Rather it means the true creative power of African people through a people's control of their forces of production and equitable distribution of the products of their sweat to enhance the quality of all their lives. Seen in this light, Black Power is impossible outside a socialist context and a total liberation of the African genius at all the levels we have been talking about. Literature, and our attitudes to literature, can help or else hinder in the creation of a united socialist Black Power in Africa based on the just continuing struggle of peasants and workers for a total control of their productive forces.

We writers and critics of African literature should form an essential intellectual part of the anti-imperialist cultural army of African peoples for total economic and political liberation from imperialism and foreign domination.

Notes

1. Paper read during a conference of teachers of literature in Kenya, at Nairobi School, in 1973.
2. 'In the world today all culture, all literature and art belong to definite classes and are geared to definite political lines. There is in fact no

such a thing as art for art's sake, art that stands above classes, art that is detached from, or independent of politics.' Mao Tse-Tung, 'Yenan Forum on Literature and Art.'

3. Arnold Hauser: 'Propaganda, Ideology and Art', *Aspects of History and Class Consciousness,* Istvan Meszaros (ed.) p. 128.
4. Ibid., p. 129.
5. Karl Marx: *Capital*, vol. 1, chap. vii, p. 177.
6. Karl Marx: 'Wage Labour and Capital', *Selected Works,* vol. 1, Moscow, p. 89.
7. 'The relations of production in their totality constitute what are called the social relations, society, and, specifically, a society at a definite stage of historical development. . . .' Karl Marx: 'Wage Labour and Capital', ibid., p. 90.
8. Friedrich Engels: *Socialism: Utopian and Scientific,* section 3.
9. 'Thus the social relations within which individuals produce, the social relations of production, change, are transformed, with the change and development of the material means of production, the productive forces.' Karl Marx: 'Wage Labour and Capital', op. cit., p. 90.
10. V. I. Lenin: *Critical remarks on the National Question,* p. 20 and p. 14.
11. Walter Rodney: *How Europe Underdeveloped Africa*, (Tanzania Publishing House, Dar-es-Salaam, 1972). See also Frank: *Capitalism and Underdevelopment in Latin America.*
12. 'Direct slavery is as much the pivot of our industrialism today as machinery, credit, etc. Without slavery no cotton; without cotton no modern industry. Slavery has given value to the colonies; the colonies have created world trade; world trade is the necessary condition of large-scale machine industry. Thus, before the traffic in Negroes began, the colonies supplied the Old World with only very few products and made no visible change in the face of the earth. Slavery is therefore an economic category of the highest importance. Without slavery North America, the most progressive country, would be transformed into a patriarchal land. You have only to wipe North America off the map of the nations and you get anarchy, the total decay of trade and of modern civilization. But to let slavery disappear is to wipe North America off the map of the nations. And therefore, because it is an economic category, we find slavery in every nation since the world began. Modern nations have merely known how to disguise slavery of their own countries while they openly imported it into the New World. Karl Marx: *The Poverty of Philosophy.'* p. 180. See also Eric Williams: *Capitalism and Slavery* (André Deutsch, London, 1964).
13. V. I. Lenin: *Imperialism, the Highest Stage of Capitalism*, (Selected Works, n.d.); and Kwame Nkrumah: *Neo-Colonialism: The Last Stage of Imperialism* (Heinemann, London, 1968).
14. Amilcar Cabral: 'National Liberation and Culture' in *Transition* 45, p. 12.

15. Quoted by Eric Williams: *History of the People of Trinidad and Tobago*, p. 30.
16. Ibid., p. 31.
17. Ibid., p. 31.
18. Quoted from Monsarrat's novel *Richer Than All His Tribe*, by Anne Dummett in *A Portrait of English Racism* p. 225—226.
19. Note the description of Gagool in *King Solomon's Mines* haunted Graham Greene all his life, at least so he says in his collected Essays. And Micere Githae Mugo has written: 'I can never forget *King Solomon's Mines* nor the weird portrait of Gagool which for a long time epitomized in my childish mind the figure of an African woman in old age. It is only recently that I have got over my dread and fear of old black women.' See her article, *Written Literature and Black Image*, in Gachukia and Akivaga's *Teaching of African Literature in Schools*.
20. See the description of this in *King Solomon's Mines*.
21. Karen Blixen: *Out of Africa*, Penguin edition, p. 24.
22. Ibid., p. 25.
23. Ibid., p. 44.
24. Isak Dinesen: *Shadows on the Grass* (John Murray, London, 1960), p. 45.
25. William Blake: 'The Little Black Boy' (*The Complete Poems*, Longman, p. 58).
26. Ibid., p. 58.
27. Mao Tse-Tung: 'Combat Liberalism'.
28. Alan Paton: *Cry the Beloved Country* (Penguin Books, Harmondsworth, 1972), p. 231—2.
29. Edward W. Blyden: 'Christianity, Islam and the Negro Race', *African Heritage Books 1*, Edinburgh, p. 77.
30. Ibid., p. 00.
31. Amilcar Cabral.
32. Nyĩmbo cia Kũinĩra Ngia, Hymn No. 115. Note that the Hymn is a Gikuyu rendering of G. Duffield's Christian hymn, 'Stand up! stand up for Jesus! Ye soldiers of the Cross'.
33. From a Gĩkũyũ song book published by Gakaara Wanjau about or just before 1952. Song No. 41.
34. Nyĩmbo cia Kũinĩra Ngia, Hymn No. 171. Original English hymn by Nahum Tate 'While shepherds watch'd their flocks by night'.
35. Gakaara Wanjaũ — Song No. 10.

2 Literature in Schools[1]

▲▲▲

The current debate about literature in our schools has shown that we Kenyans are very concerned over the literary diet now being ladled out to our children. This is as it should be. For education is 'a mirror unto' a people's social being. It has been a major ideological battlefield between the economic, political and cultural forces of oppression and the forces for national liberation and unity. Hence, the education system of us Kenyans was one of the first national fortresses to be stormed by the colonial spiritual policemen preparing and subsequently guarding the way for the permanent siege of the oppressed by all the other occupation armies of British imperialism.

The debate has raised four main issues with questions that well go beyond the problem of literature alone. These issues are as follows: (1) *The relevance and adequacy of the present education system*: What is the philosophy behind it? What are its premises and guidelines? What and whose social vision is it setting out to serve? On the basis of our answers to the above, what area and what sort of literature should we be teaching in our schools? (2) *The decision-making personnel*: Who should take crucial decisions regarding our cultural and literary programmes — foreigners or nationals? Who should determine what, and how, we are teaching in our schools? (3) *The teaching staff*: Should we still recruit and retain imperialist foreigners to teach literature, language, history and culture in our schools? Should we in fact continue employing imperialist foreigners to interpret our being to ourselves? (4) *Approaches to literature*: What is our guiding world outlook as teachers of literature? What is our attitude to literature as a reflection of society? On whose side are we when interpreting literature? To help which side in the social struggle?

The debate has tended to centre on the third issue, whether or not we should continue employing foreigners, and while this is an important matter, it has overshadowed the other three problems and has helped to obscure the main and real thrust of the report and recommendations of the working committee. The report of the committee in fact gave more space to the first two issues with comments, observations and conclusions based on the assumption that literature is a very crucial reflection of a society.

The report completely rejected the notion that a child in Nairobi can only know itself by studying London first; by first immersing itself in a European writer's imaginative responses to his countryside and to his history; the notion, in other words, that a Kenyan child's route to self-realization must be via European heritages and cultures. The price we pay for these Eurocentric studies of ourselves is the total distortion and misplacement of values of national liberation, making us continue to be slaves to imperialism.

Literature, the report argues, reflects the life of a people. It reflects in word images, a people's creative consciousness of their struggles to mould nature through co-operative labour and in the process acting on and changing themselves. It reflects in word images a people's consciousness of the tensions and conflicts arising out of their struggles to mould a meaningful social environment founded on their combined actions on nature to wrest the means of life: clothing, food and shelter. Literature thus contains people's images of themselves in history and of their place in the universe.

What images are presented to a Kenyan child through the literature he reads in Kenyan national schools? Let us be frank. Being a student of literature in today's Kenya means being an English student. Our children are taught the history of English literature and language from the unknown author of Beowulf to T. S. Eliot. They are made to recite, with ethereal faces and angelic voices, poems in praise or censure of the retiring unreachable haughtily coy mistress, a remnant of the courtly love games of the idle European feudal classes:

Go, lovely Rose!
Tell her, that wastes her time and me
That now she knows,
When I resemble her to thee,
How sweet and fair she seems to be.[2]

They recite poems which are an English writer's nostalgic response to his landscape:

I sing of brooks, of blossoms, birds and bowers:
Of April, May, of June, and July-flowers
I sing of May-poles . . .[3]

They sing of the beauty of England and of the changing seasons and flowers:

Fair daffodils, we weep to see
You haste away so soon:
As yet the early-rising sun
Has not attain'd his noon.[4]

The children are mesmerized by winter in a polluted British industrial setting and so they faithfully chant about:

The yellow fog that rubs its back upon the window-panes,
The yellow smoke that rubs its muzzle on the window-panes,
Licked its tongue into corners of the evening,
Lingered upon the pools that stand in drains,
Let fall upon its back the soot that falls from chimneys,
Slipped by the terrace, made a sudden leap,
And seeing that it was a soft October night,
Curled once about the house and fell asleep.[5]

Yes, so much for roses and daffodils and may-poles, and yellow fogs, not to mention songs of London burning and Baa Baa Black Sheep!

Thus the teaching of only European literature, and mostly British imperialist literature in our schools, means that our students are daily being confronted with the European reflection of itself, the European image, in history. Our children are made to look, analyse and evaluate the world as made and seen by Europeans. Worse still, these children are confronted with a distorted image of themselves and of their history as reflected and interpreted in European imperialist literature. They see how Prospero sees Caliban and not how Caliban sees Prospero; how Crusoe discovers and remakes Man Friday in Crusoe's image, but never how Friday views himself and his heroic struggles against centuries of Crusoe's exploitation and oppression.

This emerges more clearly if you compare literature with the state of the cinema in Kenya today. Every time we go to the movies we are confronted with the way the imperialist bourgoisie sees the world; we are faced, so to speak, with the ideological justification of their ways to themselves and to us. Thus we never see ourselves reflected on the screen; we never react to or respond to ourselves and to our environment on the screen. Worse, we often applaud the superhuman feats of racist heroes of imperialism — a James Bond or an American cowboy wiping out a whole crowd of Third World people: Africans, Chinese, Mexicans, or the native Americans — the so-called Red Indians.

This is cultural imperialism, a very powerful instrument of oppression because it distorts a people's vision of history and of the reality of the world around them. These distorted literary reflections, reinforced by religious images of white gods and angels reigning and 'choiring' in heaven while black devils writhed in hell because of their black sins, were meant to lead us — and especially the 'educated' and the Christianized — to paths of self-doubt and self-hatred and to indecisive postures before our enemies. Okot p'Bitek in *Song of Ocol* has powerfully depicted this educated generation writhing in anguish amidst tortuous thoughts and questions:

> Why
> Why was I born black?[6]

The phenomenon is not of course peculiar to Africa. It is true of the whole black world, the colonized world, indeed true of those Aimé Césaire has described as' 'Societies drained of their essence, cultures trampled underfoot, institutions undermined, lands confiscated, religions smashed, magnificent artistic creations destroyed, extraordinary possibilities wiped out.' Ocol's torments and his repudiation of the creative collective selfhood of African peoples is borne out by a real life testimony from Malcolm X who writes:

> **How ridiculous I was to stand there simply lost in admiration of my hair now looking white in the mirror. . . . This was my first really big step towards self-degradation: when**

I endured all that pain, literally burning my flesh in order
to conk my natural hair until it was limp, to have it look
like a white man's hair! I had joined that multitude of
black men and women who are brainwashed into believing
that black people are inferior and white people superior
that they will even violate and mutilate their God created
bodies to try to look pretty by white standards.[7]

Well, we may not always mutilate our bodies, but how often
have we mutilated our minds and our creative potential through
total surrender to cultural imperialism!

It is time that we realized that the European imperialist bourgeois experience of history as reflected in their art and literature
is NOT the universal experience of history. Moreover, their history has largely been one of exploitation, oppression and elimi-
nation of other peoples. Why should we, whose experiences of
history as reflected in our songs and our literature, is one of
continuous heroic struggle against western European slavery and
their imperialist pillage and plunder of our wealth, be expected
to memorize and recite the story of our imperialist oppressors
and thus identify with their literary glorification of imperialist
plunder and murder?

I am convinced that the principles guiding the report were
entirely sound: Literature of the African peoples should come
first. Literature of people who have struggled against racism,
colonialism, against imperialist economic, political and cultural
domination — and this means mostly progressive Asian and
Latin American literatures — should follow. Literature from the
rest of the world — chosen on the basis of relevance to our
struggle against inhibitive social structures — should be the third
component of literature in our schools.

In this way we shall develop a critical mentality in our students: people who can critically assess and evaluate their total
environment in Kenya and using the tools gained therefrom,
look at other worlds and similarly assess and evaluate. In literature there have been two opposing aesthetics: the aesthetic of
oppression and exploitation and of acquiescence with imperialism; and that of human struggle for total liberation. The literature
of all those who cherish and fight for freedom is our literature:
the literature of all who hate, and therefore struggle against exploitation, oppression, diminution of the human creative spirit,

is our literature: the aesthetic arising from that literature is in harmony with the aesthetic evolving from the Kenyan people's history which reached its previous highest epic peak in the Mau Mau armed struggle against British imperialism, an aesthetic which found literary expression in Mau Mau songs and poems. But the order and combination of study is important: Kenya, East Africa, Africa, Asia and Latin America, and the rest, in that order.

The second issue — the decision-making personnel — is obviously related to the first and here again the report was clear and emphatic. No independent country should allow its most vital decisions about the study of their culture to be taken by foreigners. Decisions affecting the lives of fifteen million Kenyans can only be meaningfully taken by patriotic Kenyans and not by imperialist foreigners. I don't see why this should even be a matter of debate. It is the height of criminal folly and utter national irresponsibility and naked betrayal of millions to entrust policies on national culture to foreigners. That is why the report called for the immediate Kenyanization of the inspectorates of literature and languages. I repeat: only Kenyan nationals should decide on the running of their education system.

The third issue, concerning the employment of expatriates, is dependent on what is done about the above two issues. The feeling of the working committee was that most of the current staff in our schools were recruited and employed on the basis of the current policies that have resulted in only foreign literature in our schools. A few of these teachers have no training in literature and they can only talk about backgrounds to literature, but are incapable of adequately evaluating literature, any literature, even their own, and therefore they spend time in explaining references to daffodils, wintry snow, and may-poles. Thus they hide their ignorance behind a knowledge of their language and an acquaintance with the natural and social background to the literature.

But a few of the teachers are progressive and approach literature with a sensitivity and intelligence born of a sound training and dedication to the cause of human liberation. Such are not afraid of progressive literature. They don't feel threatened by a Kenyan national literature or any other socially relevant literatures. On the contrary, these enlightened few welcome a literature whose background the students can take for granted so that

they can get on with the more exciting work of interpretation
and debate. In the same way there are a few nationals who are
authoritarian and who are obviously happier discussing and
explaining a London they know nothing about, or a Europe
learnt from imperialist literature. These literary Ocols hate this
uncivilized thing called Kenyan literature, and they also hate a
situation in which a student might be as much acquainted with
the social background as the teacher. Fortunately these Kenyans,
who are sold to the culture of imperialism without even grasp-
ing its full import are increasingly being challenged by a new
generation of Kenyan students and teachers who are committed
to a national aesthetic of liberation.

But once again, the question about the employment of
foreigners to teach literature in our schools cannot be decided
on the basis of philosophical stance of the foreigners. I believe
that only the nationals of a country have the right and the
responsibility of running their education system, and this
over-reliance on foreigners is dangerous for our country's
future.

Finally I would say that the basic assumption underlying
the committee's work and recommendations was the general
realization, as it emerged from the discussions of the main
conference, that literature, any literature, is useless unless
it is committed to the values of a people 'sceptreless and free',
developing to the highest possible level their limitless creative
potential and enjoying to the full the fruits arising therefrom.

Imperialism, in its colonial and neo-colonial stages, is the
enemy of those human values of liberation. The literature
reflecting an aesthetic that glorifies the wicked deeds of the
imperialist bourgeoisie and its local allies is enemy literature.
The literature we teach in Kenya's schools should reflect the
grandeur of our history: it should reflect Kenya's great past of
heroic struggles to overcome nature and her even more heroic
struggles against foreign domination: From the wars of resistance
against the Portuguese and the Arab slave-raiders, to the patriotic
wars against the British.

The history and the literature we teach should bring to the
fore those immortal words in Aimé Césaire's poem *Return to
My Native Land* when he argued that for a century the European
imperialist bourgeoisie has fed the colonized and the oppressed
with racist lies and defeatist propaganda.

For it is not true that the work of man is finished
That man has nothing more to do in the world

>   but be a parasite in the world

That all we now need is to keep in step with the world.

But the work of man is only just beginning and it remains
to man to conquer all the violence entrenched in the
recesses of his passion

And no race possesses the monopoly of beauty,
of intelligence, of force, and there is
a place for all at the rendezvous
of victory . . .[8]

The teaching of literature in Kenyan schools must help us to
return to our native land among the masses of Kenyan peasants
and workers, to build a self-reliant Kenya totally free from external and internal exploitation and oppression. The report of
the working committee was only a tiny tiny step in that direction. But then, the journey of a thousand miles begins with
one step.

Notes

1. This is a slightly revised article which appeared in *The Weekly Review*,
   1976 as part of the fierce debate which erupted in Kenya's press after a
   working committee appointed by the conference of teachers of literature, Nairobi School, 1973 to re-examine the literature syllabus in
   schools, released its findings and recommendations in a document
   entitled: *Teaching of Literature in Kenya's Secondary Schools.*
2. Edmund Waller, 'Go Lovely Rose!', in Read and Dobree, *The London
   Book of English Verse.*
3. Robert Herrick, 'Argument of His Book'.
4. Robert Herrick, 'Daffodils', in Read and Dobree, *op. cit.*
5. T. S. Eliot, 'The Love Song of Alfred Prufrock', *The Complete Poems
   and Plays of T. S. Eliot* (Faber, London, 1969), p. 13.
6. Okot p'Bitek, *Song of Ocol* (EAPH, Nairobi, 1970), p. 22.
7. The Autobiography of Malcolm X.
8. Aimé Césaire, *Return to My Native Land* (Penguin, Haemondsworth,
   1969), p. 85.

3 Kenyan Culture
: The National Struggle for Survival

▲▲▲

A central fact of Kenyan life today is the fierce struggle between the cultural forces representing foreign interests and those representing patriotic national interests. This cultural struggle may not always be obvious to a casual observer, for such a person will almost certainly be struck by the virtual domination of Kenyan life by foreigners and foreign imperialist cultural interests.

If such an observer should want to see a film show, he will be sitting in cinemas owned by foreigners (Twentieth Century Fox for instance) to see American offerings on the screen. These offerings range from the moderately good like *Coming Home*, which was slightly critical of American imperialist adventurism in Indo-China; to the mass-produced, mindless trash like *Omen* and *Magic* where change, and possibilities of change, are seen in terms of doomsday and the end of human civilization. The message is clear: any change from the American dominated present is the end of civilization. Agents of change are devils. The heroes (all American of course) are those fighting against the villains from Hades or outer space who threaten the present world stability guaranteed by American dollars and guns.

Should the same visitor want to buy a daily newspaper, his choice is between the Nation Newspapers owned by the Aga Khan in Paris, or the Standard Newspapers owned by Tiny Rowland's Lonrho in London. Thus the two major means of mass communication to Kenya's reading public are owned by foreign imperialist firms. The editors may be Kenyans. But when there is a conflict between the editorial policy and that of the foreign owner, it is the interests of the Kenyans which must give way.

If our visitor should want to see book publishing houses in

Kenya, he will be welcomed by Kenyan directors of branches of such well known foreign firms like Heinemann, Longman, Oxford, Nelson, Macmillan and the like. The only exception is the Kenya government-owned Kenya Literature Bureau. These firms sometimes publish books written by Kenyans. But it means that book production, both in quantity and quality, is at the grace and mercy of foreigners.

Now our visitor might visit schools. The English language dominates a Kenyan child's life from primary school to university and after. Swahili, the all-Kenya national language, is not only *not* compulsory, but is often offered as an optional alternative to French and German. There is total neglect of the languages of the nationalities that make up Kenya. Thus a Kenyan child grows up admiring the culture carried by these foreign languages, in effect western European ruling class cultures, and looks down upon the culture carried by the language of his particular nationality, in effect Kenyan peasant rooted national cultures. In other words, the school trains him to look down upon what is national and Kenyan, and to look up to what is foreign even if it is anti-Kenyan. This process is hastened by the literature he is made to study: Shakespeare, Jane Austen, and Wordsworth still dominate the literary scene in Kenyan schools. The present language situation in Kenya means that over ninety per cent of Kenyans (mostly peasants) are completely excluded from participation in national debates conducted in the written word.

The trend is virtually the same in music and the plastic arts. It is either foreign music, or Kenyan music but produced by foreign firms. It is either foreign sculpture and painting, or Kenyan sculpture and painting but exhibited in foreign-owned art galleries.

But it is in the theatre that this domination by foreign cultural interests is most nakedly clear. Nairobi has recently seen a mushrooming of neo-colonial foreign cultural institutions like the French Cultural Centre, the German Goethe Institute; the Japanese Cultural Institute, and of course the American Information Services. Some of these institutes promote theatre and theatre-related events and discussions. But naturally they are basically interested in selling a positive image of their governments' neo-colonial profit-hunting adventurism in Asia, Africa and Latin America.

A most ludicrous colonial affair is the Donovan Maule Theatre in Nairobi. With their productions like *The Killing of Sister George* and Michael Frayn's *Clouds*, they see themselves as offering a touch of civilization (West End and Broadway combined) in theatrically darkest Africa. One of their favourite advertisements in tourist brochures is the supposedly dramatic slogan: *A Professional Theatre in the Heart of Africa*. They just about avoided advertising a professional theatre in the Heart of Darkness!

What really annoys most patriotic Kenyans about the theatre scene in their own country is not so much the above foreign presences but the fact that the Kenya government-owned premises, The Kenya Cultural Centre and The Kenya National Theatre, should themselves be controlled by foreigners offering foreign theatre to Kenyans. A foreign imperialist cultural mission, i.e. The British Council, occupies virtually all the offices at The Kenya Cultural Centre. The governing council of the same Centre is chaired by a British national and The British Council is in addition represented on the council. The Kenya National Theatre which is run by the governing council is completely dominated by foreign-based theatre groups like The City Players and Theatre Ltd. What these groups offer has nothing to do with Kenyan life except when maybe they offer racist shows like *The King and I* or *Robinson Crusoe*. A small list of titles they offer is quite revealing: *A Funny Thing Happened on the Way to the Forum; Godspell; Jesus Christ Superstar; Oklahoma; Carmen; Vivat! Vivat Regina!* etc. Most of these groups at The Kenya National Theatre often import directors, costumes, orchestral pieces and actors from England and Canada, giving the impression that there are no Kenyan directors, no Kenyan costumes, no Kenyan actors and no Kenyan musical instruments. As for the theatre critics (again foreigners) their critical vocabulary is a variation of three sentences: 'It is universal'; or 'It is not talking about oppression'; or 'It has a touch of West End or Broadway'. The Kenyan reply to all this over the years has met with varying degrees of success and failure.

In the cinema there has not been any success. A Kenyan film-maker, Hilary Ng'weno, once tried entering the field only to make an exit for lack of financial backing and lack of venues. Kenya television would rather import films about the American Wild West than encourage a modest Kenyan effort.

In the newspaper world, various Kenyan enterprises like *The Nairobi Evening News* and *The Weekend Star* have flared up for a day only to disappear the following day for lack of advertisements from the mostly foreign firms in Kenya; for lack of adequate capital and also because of the severe restraint of a self-imposed censorship for fear of overstepping the boundaries. The only Kenyan-owned enterprise which has so far survived is Hilary Ng'weno's *Weekly Review* and *The Nairobi Times*. The *Weekly Review*, for instance, has been in print for four years. Their content and outlook however is entirely another matter.

The Kenyan-owned publishing industry has not fared any better, with groups rising and falling for similar reasons: lack of adequate capital, or inadequate government patronage.

In the schools, a conference of Kenyan teachers of literature met in 1973 and for the next three years or so produced far-reaching, detailed recommendations on the teaching of literature in Kenyan schools, basically asking the Kenyan government to replace the present syllabus, whose centre is foreign imperialist culture, with one which would be Kenyan and African based. The recommendations went through all the necessary administrative organs, often meeting with enthusiastic approval, until the time of implementation; they have now been shelved. Jane Austen is certainly deemed more relevant to Kenya than Chinua Achebe.

Kenyan musicians, like Joseph Kamaru, are struggling against great odds but they have survived and continue to enliven the Kenyan musical scene with their compositions in Kenyan national languages, thus reaching a mass audience.

But once again, it is in the theatre where the struggle for national expression in culture is most manifest. Kenyan drama groups like the Festac 77 Drama Group which produced Ngũgĩ and Mĩcere Mũgo's *The Trial of Dedan Kĩmathi* and Imbuga's *Betrayal in the City*; The University of Nairobi Free Travelling Theatre which tours all over Kenya once a year with a repertoire of plays in Kiswahili and English; The Tamaduni Players and The Kenya National Theatre Company; the Kenyan Schools and Colleges Drama Festivals; have all tried to challenge this foreign establishment in theatre. In the process, they have unleashed a torrent of Kenyan talents in acting and directing that puts to shame the foreign productions.

And yet often these talented Kenyans have no venue for their theatrical performances. Often these Kenyan groups of amateurs have to go cap in hand to imperialist cultural institutes, like the French Cultural Centre, to beg for stage facilities because there is no room in the ark for them at their own national premises. Very occasionally they may get a night or two at The Kenya National Theatre, but only in the months when the foreign European groups are resting.

One of the weaknesses of these various national efforts is that writers, directors and actors often operate within the same tradition as the foreign theatre they are setting out to challenge. First, their theatre has mostly been in a foreign language, i.e. English, and therefore, despite any radical innovations in content and method, their main target audience can only be the foreign, English-speaking audience or the urban, Kenyan English-speaking bourgeoisie. These groups have tried to exploit the resources of the Kenyan national languages (that is the languages of the several nationalities that make up Kenya) and the cultural traditions carried by these languages. Hence these groups despite their achievements in what is a difficult situation have not yet appealed to a truly national audience; that is the peasants and workers who form the overwhelming human content of Kenya both in terms of numbers and in the production of Kenya's wealth and, more importantly, who have for the last seven decades stood opposed to foreign interference and oppression.

Most of the Kenyan writers for theatre have not tried to represent this last point or even tried to change the content of their drama to take militantly patriotic stands. Their plays have espoused the same class, sometimes the same racist values, of their Western foreign counterparts. A good example is Kenneth Watene's *Dedan Kimathi* which depicts Kimathi, the brilliant Mau Mau guerrila leader against the British colonial presence, in the same terms as he was last depicted by racist Ian Henderson in *The Hunt for Dedan Kimathi* twenty years ago. Because they have operated within the same structure of values, assumptions, political outlook, language audience, as the foreign theatre establishment, most of these groups have not been able to make a very effective challenge to imperialist cultural domination in Kenya. The three exceptions are: The Schools and Colleges Drama Festival; The University of Nairobi Free Travelling Theatre; The Festac 77 Drama Group.

This is the historical importance of the emergence of village-based theatre groups like that of Kamĩrĩĩthũ Community Education and Cultural Centre in Limuru. This group in 1977 produced *Ngaahika Ndeenda* by Ngũgĩ wa Thiong'o and Ngugi wa Mĩrĩi, the first major modern play in one of Kenya's languages. The actors were all peasants and workers from Kamĩrĩĩthũ village, they designed and built an open-air stage in the centre of the village, and they collaborated in the evolution of the script as well as in the directing. In the process they broke with the hitherto accepted theatrical traditions. For instance the initial reading and discussion of the script was done in the open. The selection of actors was done in the open with the village audience helping in the selection, and all the rehearsals for four months were done in the open with an ever increasing crowd of commentators and directors. The dress rehearsal was done to an audience of over one thousand peasants and workers. When finally the show opened to a fee-paying audience, the group performed to thousands of peasants and workers who often would hire buses or trek on foot in order to come and see the play. For the first time, the rural people could see themselves and their lives and their history portrayed in a positive manner. For the first time in their post-independence history a section of the peasantry had broken out of the cruel choice that was hitherto their lot: the Bar or the church. And not the least, they smashed the racialist view of peasants as uncultured recipients of cultures from beneficient foreigners.

The withdrawal of the licence to perform the play and the subsequent detention of one of the authors in December 1977 was a severe blow to the efforts of some Kenyans to successfully challenge the foreign theatre and cultural establishment in Kenya, and the efforts of Kenyans to positively affirm themselves in theatre and culture. It also betrayed the blatantly accomplice role played by important sections of the Kenyan ruling elements and showed where perhaps the real opposition lay.

Despite this temporary setback, Kamĩrĩĩthũ's example provided the first meaningful challenge to imperialist cultural domination in Kenya by changing the whole terms of the struggle — in location, audience, language, values, and even style of production, i.e. the communal participation.

It seems to me that the choice in Kenya today is between the foreign imperialist-type theatre in foreign languages, and the national patriotic efforts like those of the peasants and workers of Kamĩrĩĩthũ Community Education and Cultural Centre in Kenya's own national languages. The two positions are irreconcilable because they represent two opposed class interests: anti-Kenyan and foreign; and pro-Kenyan, patriotic and national. The first choice can only lead Kenya to cultural sterility and death; the second would lead Kenya to cultural regeneration and strength, national pride and dignity.

In making their choice, the Kenyan people may want to look back to history and realize that no civilization on earth has ever thrived on blind imitation and copying; that foreigners, no matter how well intentioned, no matter how clever and gifted, no matter how original, can never develop our culture and our languages for us. It is only patriotic Kenyans who can develop Kenyan culture and languages. Only a culture which is a product of our people's history, and which in turn correctly reflects that history, can push Kenya to the forefront in the community of nations. It is such a culture which can help us build a modern human civilization free from the *social cannibalism* which today has reduced over three-quarters of mankind to beggary, poverty and death, not because they don't work but because their wealth goes to feed, clothe and shelter a few idle classes in America, western Europe and Japan.

In the present cultural struggle between imperialist and national interests, most Kenyans would take the view that a modern Kenyan national culture should reflect the strength and confidence of a people who have completely rejected the position of always being the *ragged trousered philanthropists* to money-mongers in London and New York and in the other western seats of barons of the profits snatched from the peasants and workers of the world.

Notes

1. An article commissioned by *The Guardian* in its commemorative issue of 7 June 1979 in honour of President Moi's state visit to Britain.

4 'Handcuffs' for a Play[1]
(or the difficulties of staging a Kenyan play on Kenyatta Day)

▲▲

The recent announcement that *The Trial of Dedan Kĩmathi* and *Betrayal in the City* will run for eight nights at The Kenya National Theatre between 20 to 30 October has raised awkward questions among Kenyan theatre-goers. Why have the two plays, which will be representing Kenya in Lagos, been crammed into four nights each between two European shows, Bossman's *Jeune Ballet de France* (10 to 18 October), and the City Players' *A Funny Thing Happened on the Way to the Forum* (1 to 21 November)?

This means that, between them, the two foreign cultural shows will have a total of thirty-one days at The National Theatre while the two Kenyan plays will have only eight days. Surely the people of this country have a right to see and to criticise over a period of time, what will be representing them at the Second World Black and African Festival of Arts and Culture in Lagos, Nigeria?

What the public may not know is that since June, 1976 there has been a bitter struggle between the Kenyan Festac '77 Drama Group and the management of The Kenya National Theatre over what plays and what events should be on at the Kenya Cultural Centre during the Kenyatta Day week and also during the Unesco General Conference to be hosted by Kenya.

Kenya Festac '77 Drama Group (the name under which the Drama Sub-Committee of the Ministry of Social Services is organising the two Kenyan plays) insisted that *The Trial of Dedan Kĩmathi* and *Betrayal in the City* should be performed during the Kenyatta Day week and for another week or so during the Unesco Conference. Under the chairmanship of Seth Adagala, the group argued that the Kenyatta Day week and indeed the whole of October was very crucial in the history of

Kenya. It was after all, the month in which some Mau Mau and KAU leaders were arrested and detained. It was the month in which the Mau Mau armed struggle against British colonialism started. What could be more relevant for the week than a play about one of the most heroic leaders of the Mau Mau armed resistance? Kenyans needed to remind themselves that their independence had been won through sweat and blood.

The foreign management, on the other hand, were for Bossman's *Jeune Ballet de France* and the City Players' *A Funny Thing Happened on the Way to the Forum*. Their only argument was that the dates had been booked many months ago; that African plays never attracted true theatre-lovers anyway. Statistics were even quoted as evidence. They never stopped to ask why, even assuming their allegations to be true, there was a small audience for African plays at The National Theatre. Couldn't the reason be found in the fact that African plays were always crammed into two or three nights and therefore gaining very little from the crucial word-of-mouth publicity given by the first three nights' audiences? Couldn't it also be that The National Theatre has, over the years, created the image of a service station for irrelevant cultural shows such as *Godspell*, *The Boyfriend*, *Jeune Ballet de France*, *A Funny Thing Happened on the Way to the* [Roman] *Forum*?

At issue behind the struggle over dates were basic questions of principle. Shouldn't The Kenya National Theatre and the Kenya Cultural Centre be catering for national interests? In planning cultural activities for the year, didn't the theatre management take the Kenyan image in and outside the country into consideration? What shows should be organised for national festivals like Madaraka Week, Kenyatta, Jamhuri Day, Labour Day, etc?

There were also certain symbolic parallels in the subject-matter of at least *The Trial of Dedan Kimathi* and the venue, i.e. The National Theatre, and the history of this country.

It is interesting, for instance, that The National Theatre was opened in 1952 under a colonial management. Many of the plays they performed between 1952 and 1958 served to entertain the British soldiers who came to Kenya to fight against Mau Mau guerrillas and to suppress the Kenyan people. Such colonial theatre was meant to boost the morale of British soldiers, while at the same time taking captive the minds and hearts of the educated Kenyan African petty bourgeois. Over the same period, the Mau Mau guerillas led by Dedan Kĩmathi and others put up one of the most heroic armed struggles against imperialism in this century. It is often forgotten that while liberation movements in places such as Guinea Bissau, Mozambique, Angola and Algeria had free neighbouring territories which served as supply and operation bases, the Mau Mau guerrillas had no such bases. They were surrounded by the enemy administration and so they had to entirely depend on what arms they could steal from the enemy and what guns they could make in the nascent underground arms factories in the cities and forests. The Mau Mau guerrillas also developed a strong anti-imperialist national culture, as seen in their written literature and in their songs created on the battlefield. *The Trial of Dedan Kĩmathi* tries to recapture the heroism and the determination of the people in this glorious moment of Kenya's history, a moment that was the culmination of struggles that were started by other national resistance heroes such as Waiyaki, Me Katilili, Koitalel, etc., at the turn of the century.

The fact that the Ministry of Social Services had to intervene before these two plays were allowed to run at The National Theatre shows the extent to which theatre and our cultural institutions are in the hands of foreigners — mostly British — whose only aim is to promote British imperialist interests in the country. At a time when theatre in Kenya is trying to reflect national history and a national struggle, the foreign management of our Cultural Centre is selling Christmas cards that commemorate The National Theatre as it was in 1952, flying a colonial flag. It is very insulting that The Kenya National Theatre in 1976 should be selling a Christmas card carrying the British flag!

However, despite their production being crammed between two foreign productions, the Kenya Festac '77 Drama Group, led by directors Seth Adagala and Tirus Gathwe, seem determined to do their best. They are encouraged by the support they have had from the Kenyan people, says Seth Adagala. 'We are determined to make a hit in Lagos. We shall represent Kenya and represent her well, despite some frustrations.'

As for me, I think the birth of the Kenya Festac '77 Drama Group, which for the first time has brought together Kenya's writers, artists, directors, actors and producers, from all walks of life ranging from the University to insurance companies, has added to the growth of a patriotic national theatre arts movement that is developing in fierce struggle against imperialist theatre and cultures.

No foreigner can hold back this movement. It's only fitting that this national arts movement will make yet another milestone on Kenyatta Day with the performance of *The Trial of Dedan Kīmathi* which celebrates the uncompromising heroic leadership of Kīmathi. Seth Adagala and Tirus Gathwe are looking forward to big public support. Judging by the enthusiastic response to the University of Nairobi Free Travelling Theatre, which shows that the people want a theatre reflecting national culture and national life, the two directors should have no difficulty in filling the theatre — for the four days allowed to each between 20 October and 30 October.

Notes

1. An article that appeared in the *Daily Nation* of 15 October, 1976, just before the opening of *The Trial of Dedan Kīmathi* at The Kenya National Theatre in October, 1976. All the shows were sold out, with some people travelling from as far as Kisumu, Nyeri and Mombasa to see the play.

5 Return to the Roots

**National Languages as the Basis of a
Kenya National Literature and Culture[1]**

In 1958, a year after Ghana's independence, a young Nigerian writer, Chinua Achebe, published his first novel, *Things Fall Apart*, and it gave rise to a literary stream still flowing out of the pens of numerous African writers.

Most of the works produced by these pens have different subject-matter: for instance, some of the novels, plays and poems have a strong anti-imperialist content while others are completely insensitive to imperialism as a social historical force in Africa today. Even to the same subject-matter the authors have assumed differing attitudes and postures. Some have a content which shows the reality of the struggles of peasants and workers of Africa against their ruthless exploitation by an alliance of foreign money-mongers in Tokyo, Bonn, Paris, London, New York and local money-mongers and holders of moneyed privileges, while others have a content that masks the reality of the struggle, a content that would send us into sweet slumber murmuring to ourselves: *Oh how beautiful the First Bank of Chicago/New York Building is lying side by side with International Life House and the Hilton all in peace and harmony with Mathare Valley, oh our City in the sun*; a content, if you like, which sets out to persuade us that producing ten million-aires of the sweat of ten million hungry shelterless, clothe-less peasants and workers is development.

But from *Things Fall Apart* in the fifties to *Petals of Blood* in the seventies, nearly all the novels, poems and plays have been written in foreign languages: this is their one unifying factor.

To choose a language is to choose a world, once said a West Indian thinker, and although I do not share the assumed primacy of language over the world, the choice of a language already pre-determines the answer to the most important question for producers of imaginative literature: For whom do I write? Who is my audience? If you write in a foreign language, French for instance, you can only reach a French-speaking audience; if in English, an English-speaking audience; in practice, foreigners and those of your people who know that foreign language. If a Kenyan writer writes in English — no matter how radical the content of that literature — he cannot possibly reach or directly talk to the peasants and workers of Kenya. If a Kenyan acts a play in English (or in French as it is now becoming the fashion) he cannot possibly be assuming a truly Kenyan audience.

The question of audience has a bearing on the next few problems for a writer: What is the subject and content of my works? From whose standpoint do I look at that content, whether I am critical of the content or not? You cannot possibly write for a peasant-worker audience (or perform) the same things in the same way as you would for the parasitic jet set in Africa. The bourgeois class wants a literature that titillates the senses, that makes them pass through Mathare Valley without seeing it. For them sex and more sex is the answer; or else, absurd little sugary, musical left-overs from abroad which are so fashionable in Kenyan theatres: bartered pride for peace of mind over a glass of whisky? Tell this class that their water is taken from the mouth of the thirsty, their clothes from bodies of naked children, awaken them from their sweet self-deceitful slumbers, and you might find yourself in a maximum security prison. On the other hand, if you write in a language understood by peasants and workers (and thus assuming them as the audience), you'll have to search your literary conscience whether to correctly reflect their lives or not; whether to tell them their poverty is God-ordained or man-conditioned and therefore to be fought.

The position of the African writer who has chosen total dependence on, and literary enslavement to, foreign languages and who at the same time wants to speak to a national audience, can be compared to that of the following characters that I have met, one in Limuru, and the others in Nakuru.

In 1966, a girl from my village, Kamĩrĩĩthũ, in Limuru, went to England to train as a nurse. She was about twenty. She stayed in England for two years. When she returned to our village, she spoke to the crowd of peasants who had gathered to welcome her through an interpreter. Rumour went that even to her parents she could only communicate through an interpreter.

A two-year stay in England had apparently wiped out her twenty years' knowledge of her mother tongue.

A few years back I went to visit a friend at Nakuru. That was before Nakuru became so famous in contemporary Kenya's political vocabulary. A man and his wife and their seven year old daughter joined us on the verandah. I knew the man and his wife because they and I were once students at Makerere and were active in anti-colonial activities. The following scene unfolds:

Mother goads daughter to speak. Daughter speaks in English. Mother then urges daughter to read a book. She obliges with an English book: I think *Winnie the Pooh* or something. I make the mistake of speaking to daughter in Gĩkũyũ. Daughter answers with a stream of incomprehensible words. Mother laughs with pride. Then she puts on a very sad face: 'Children of these days! They don't know our native tongues. Only English, English all the time, so different from our times, don't you think?'

You could see that mother and father were really proud not only that their daughter could speak English with an upper class English accent, but that she could also *not* speak Gĩkũyũ at all. Thus ignorance of the language of her own nationality, instead of being a matter for personal shame and discomfort became a thing for positive pride.

Faced with accusations that he has abandoned his national languages for foreign languages, the African writer has oscillated between the position of the girl-nurse and that of the mother and child.

Let me give a few concrete examples: In 1963 a Nigerian critic, Obi Wali, wrote an article for *Transition* magazine in which he argued that African literature as then understood and practised was merely a minor appendage in the mainstream of European literature:

> The whole uncritical acceptance of English and French as the inevitable medium of educated African writing is misdirected and has no chance of advancing African literature and culture. In other words, until these writers and their western midwives accept the fact that any true African literature must be written in African languages, they would be merely pursuing a dead end, which can only lead to sterility, uncreativity, and frustration . . . (African literature lacks any *blood and stamina*) because it is severely

limited to the European-orientated few college graduates in the new universities of Africa, steeped as they are in European literature and culture.

The ordinary local audience with little or no education in the conventional European manner and who constitute an overwhelming majority has no chance of participating in this kind of literature.[2]

This article aroused a lot of wrath from African writers: Wole Soyinka, who currently is advocating Swahili as a continental language, disdainfully demanded to know 'what Obe Wali has done to translate my plays or others into Ibo or whatever language he professes to speak.'[3] Chinua Achebe was later to write defiantly that he had been 'given the language and I intend to use it'.

Ezekiel Mphahlele, for a long time regarded as a leading critic of African literature, was even more forthright in his total embrace of the English language, in fact ascribing to it mystical political powers:

English and French have become the common languages with which to present a nationalistic front against white oppressors. Where the white man has already retreated as in the independent states, these two languages are still a unifying force.[4]

Turning to South Africa, Mphahlele criticized the fascist regime for encouraging 'vernacular' languages:

. . . the (S.A.) government has decreed that the African languages shall be used as the medium of instruction right up to secondary schools. The aim is obviously to arrest the black man's education because the previous systems whereby English was the medium for the first six years of primary education produced a strong educated class that has in turn given us a sophisticated class of political leaders and a sophisticated following — a real threat to white supremacy.[5]

Mphahlele could not see that the South African government did not want English, not because of any mystical political qualities inherent in the language, but because of the uncensored wide range of reading material readily available in that language. With the government control of publishing houses in African languages the government hoped to control the content of what people would read in those languages. For Mphahlele, English was politically superior to African languages. The sophisticated leadership that he talked about had to wait for SOWETO school-children to show them the correct path of resistance to fascism.

The position of Mphahlele has been echoed by Professor Ali Mazrui in all his writings on the English language. In his book *Cultural Engineering and Nation Building in East Africa*[6] for instance, he tends to argue that it was English language, English literature, and English culture in that order that created nation-alism in East Africa.

Another African writer Taban lo Liyong, in his book *The Last Word*[7] tells us that since his father was opposed to Taban talking English at university, Taban lo Liyong was very happy when he received news of his father's death: he could now study English in freedom.

And finally I can remember I myself, in 1965 or 1966 in the deepest ignorance of my colonial education, writing a talk on English as a second language for the BBC European language programme, in which I outlined the advantages of writing in English as opposed to writing in African languages. One of the reasons I gave was that English had a large vocabulary!

Thus the position of most African writers is not very different from that of foreign critics like Gerald Moore for instance, who once commended the creative intelligence of Africans for choos-ing the English language as the medium of their literary produc-tion. His book on African literature was appropriately titled: *The Chosen Tongue*,[8] meant of course to echo the Biblical notion of the chosen people. The English language was thus seen as the God chosen tongue in the same way as the Israelites saw themselves as the God chosen race on earth.

The major failing in Obi Wali's article was its ignoring the issue of imperialism. He could not see, or if he did he failed to stress the point, that the root cause of the African writer's predicament was historically explainable in terms of the colonial/racist encirclement and brutal suppression of African languages and cultures; that the African writer was himself part of the petty-bourgeois class which had completely imbibed, or had been made to imbibe, western bourgeois education and cultures and the world outlook these carried; a petty-bourgeois class which, if and when it saw the necessity of rebellion, tended to see that rebellion only within the same inherited tradition of language and culture.

I do not of course want to suggest that the writers I have quoted above still cling to the same views on national and foreign languages. They may, in fact, have changed their positions. I certainly have changed mine.

But the fact still remains that none of the African writers were able to satisfactorily answer Obi Wali's challenge, because the only way in which they could have meaningfully met the challenge was through a conscious deliberate rejection of their class base, and their total identification with the position of peasants and workers in their struggle against exploitation by an alliance of the imperialist bourgeoisie and the *comprador* bourgeoisie to end all forms of exploitation, oppression and domination. They would then have had to put all their intellectual resources into the service of the peasant/worker struggles not by haranguing the ruling class, appealing if you like to its conscience, but by giving correct images of the struggle for the direct consumption of the only alliance that matters in Africa's historic struggle for its dignity; the alliance of workers and peasants.

Instead, the petty-bourgeois African writers heaped one indignity upon another on the African peasant and worker characters necessitated by the very choice of language and audience. Often the African peasant characters were made to appear naïve and simple-minded because of the kind of simplistic, distorted foreign languages through which they were made to articulate their feelings and world outlook. More often the peasant/worker characters were given the vacillating mentality and pessimistic world outlook of the petty bourgeois. But the final indignity was that even where the peasant/worker characters were given their due in terms of dignity and world outlook, they were made to express these awkwardly in foreign languages. Thus the tongues of millions of peasants were mutilated in the works of African writers, and in their stead the peasants were given plastic surgery in the literary laboratories of Africa and emerged with English, French and Portuguese tongues. The final indignity consisted precisely in this death wish for an

African-language speaking peasantry and working class and the literary creation of a foreign-language speaking peasantry and working class.

I do not wish of course to ascribe any mystical qualities to the mere fact of writing in African languages without regard to content and form. But the questions Obi Wali posed about peasant/worker audiences as the strongest source of stamina and blood for African literature is basic and primary, and Kenyan writers in particular must meet the challenge of language choice and audience before we can meaningfully talk of a national literature and a national theatre as two of the most important roots of a modern Kenyan national culture.

What in fact has so far been produced by Kenyan writers in English is *not* African literature at all. It is *Afro-Saxon literature*, part of that body of literature produced by African writers in foreign languages like French, Portuguese, Italian, Spanish, that we should correctly term: *Afro-European literature*.

Kenyan national literature should mostly be produced in the languages of the various nationalities that make up modern Kenya. Kenyan national literature can only get its stamina and blood by utilizing the rich national traditions of culture and history carried by the languages of all the Kenyan nationalities. In other words, Kenyan national literature can only grow and thrive if it reaches for its roots in the rich languages, cultures and history of the Kenyan peasant masses who are the majority class in each of the Kenya's several nationalities.

Let me, for a moment dwell on this: a language, any language, has its social base in a people's production of their material life — in the practical activity of human beings co-operating and communicating in labour to wrestle with nature to procure their material means of life — food, clothing and shelter. Language as a system of verbal signposts is a product of a people communicating in labour, that is their production, exchange and distribution of wealth. Languages arise historically as a social need.

But over time, a particular system of verbal signposts comes to reflect a given people's historical consciousness of their twin struggles over nature and over the social product. Their language becomes the memory-bank of their collective struggles over a period of time. Language thus comes to embody both continuity and change in that historical consciousness. It is this aspect of language, as a collective memory-bank of a given people, which has made some people ascribe mystical independence to language. It is the same aspect which has made nations and peoples take up arms to prevent a total annihilation or assimilation of their languages, because it is tantamount to annihilating that people's collective memory-bank of past achievements and failures which form the basis of their common identity. It is like uprooting that community from history.

> History is nothing but the succession of the separate generations, each of which exploits the materials, the capital funds, the productive forces handed down to it by all preceeding generations, and thus, on the one hand, continues the traditional activity in completely changed circumstances, and on the other, modifies the old circumstances with a completely changed activity. (Karl Marx).[9]

Language is both a product of that succession of the separate generations, as well as being a banker of the way of life — culture — reflecting those modifications of collective experience in production. Literature as a process of thinking in images utilizes language and draws upon the collective experience — history — embodied in that language. In writing one should hear all the whispering, and the shouting and crying and the loving and the hating of the many voices in the past and those voices will never speak to a writer in a foreign language.

For we Kenyan writers can no longer avoid the question: Whose language and history will our literature draw upon? Foreign languages and the history and cultures carried by those languages? Or national languages — Dholuo, Kiswahili, Gĩkũyũ, Luluhya, Kikamba, Kimasai, Kigiriama, etc., — and the histories and cultures carried by those languages?

The questions bring us back to the issue of audience. If a Kenyan writer wants to speak to the peasants and workers then he should write in the languages they speak; i.e. in the languages of the Kenyan nationalities or in the all-Kenya national language which is Kiswahili. If, on the other hand, he wants to communicate with foreigners and those that speak the foreign tongues, he must use foreign languages like English, French and German. If a Kenyan writer wants to be part of the Kenya national main stream, seeking inspiration and strength from the many national voices past and present, then he should utilize national languages. But if he wants to be part of a foreign main stream seeking inspiration and strength from foreign voices, then he should use foreign languages. In making their choice, Kenyan writers should remember that the struggle of Kenyan national languages against domination by foreign languages is part of the wider historical struggle of the Kenyan national culture against imperialist domination.

In a very informative paper entitled *Language and Politics in Kenya*, Dr Karega Mutahi has pointed out that between 1900 and 1940, the British colonial government in Kenya was broadly hostile to many Kenyans learning English because of the same kind of fear, as we noted in the case of South African fascist regime, that some radical progressive literature, and especially anti-imperialist communist literature available in English, might be accessible to Kenyans. But by 1950, the need to consciously create and foster a native bourgeois class with British imperialist bourgeois values to cater for British interests in the future Kenya had outweighed the other fear of easy accessibility of radical anti-imperialist literature, and it was decided that English should be taught at the expense of Kiswahili. I quote Mutahi:

The political unity of denying English to Africans had ceased to exist. Politically the situation demanded that Africans be taught the language. Reasons for this sudden change can be found in a speech given by the Governor Sir Phillip Mitchell in Nairobi in 1954. He said: . . . what we have set our hands here is the establishment of a civilized state in which the values and standards are to be the values and the standards of Britain, in which everyone whatever his origins, has an interest and a part. The wildest naked man in Turkana has an investment in it, although apart from the security he now enjoys, it may be a remotely maturing one. . . .

From the above it is obvious that in establishing British values and standards in Kenya, African elites were needed. It was only with such an elite class that those values could be entrenched in this country. The teaching of English to Africans must be seen as a process of safeguarding European interests in Kenya. This was to be done by making sure that these Africans had the same views and culture as their colonial masters.[10]

It is therefore not accidental that at the same time as the English language was being used as a tool to forge bourgeois unity in Kenya, other cultural institutions for spreading British imperialist interests were started: the Outward Bound Movement to school Kenyans in a British Scout mountaineering mentality; cinemas like Theatre Royal, Capitol, Empire, and playhouse cinemas run by Sir Ernest Vasey's New Theatres Ltd., to show British films; the Nairobi Musical Society and the East African Conservatoire of Music given land to promote British and western music in Kenya; the British Forces' Broadcasting Unit of the then cable and wireless studios at Kabete organized entertainment by and for Africans under the direction of Peter Colmore and the settler leader, Michael Blundell.

But one of the most important institutions was the theatre. The Donovon Maule Theatre Ltd., was started in 1948 in Nairobi; the Kenya National Theatre was built in 1952 with the then Governor Sir Phillip Mitchell as one of the directors of the governing council; the Little Theatre Club was started in Mombasa in 1952; and similar amateur theatre clubs were started all over Kenya, in Nakuru and Eldoret for instance. All these were meant to promote British, English language theatre in Kenya. This British imperialist cultural offensive in Kenya, consciously and deliberately launched in the 1950s at the same time as the outbreak of Mau Mau war of national independence, continues unabated to the present time.

If you are in doubt, you only have to open the pages of any Kenyan newspaper on the entertainment pages to see what theatre the foreign groups who have controlled the so-called Kenyan National Theatre since its inception in 1952 are showing there, seventeen full years after independence. It is all foreign theatre glorifying the deeds of foreigners. *Oklohoma; The Bartered Bride; The King and I; Why Not Stay for Breakfast?* and other theatrical activities in the same vein. What have these to do with struggles in Kenya? Everything. For they are part of the imperialist culture suppressing Kenyan national cultures. Lest we forget, only as recently as 1975 was Annabel Maule made a Member of the British Empire for promoting British theatre in Kenya since 1948. Again, you have only to open the same pages and read the theatre arts column to see some of these racist foreign critics calling Kenyan patriots like Dedan Kĩmathi terrorists, and praising to the sky plays that depict the likes of Kĩmathi as sex-motivated, senseless terrorists. For such critics, any play that does *not* say anything about colonial oppression is good: any play that is anti-imperialist is bad theatre. Do you think that all this is an accident? No. It is part of a great cultural military design against the minds and hearts of Kenyans.

At the same time as the English language was being encouraged and the British bourgeois culture carried by that language was being promoted, Kenyan national languages were being actively discouraged and the progressive culture they carried, actively suppressed.

According to Dr Karega Mũtahi in the paper quoted above, African languages either during the colonial presence or during independence have never been given more than lip service. Some have never been reduced to writing. During the colonial presence between 1900 and 1963, some of these languages were taught for the first four years of primary education to meet the needs of missionaries (to be able to read the Bible) and to be able to read colonial instructions. But after independence, even this little tribute to Kenyan languages was dropped by the English-speaking bourgeois class that had received the flag from the British imperialist bourgeoisie.

Again between 1909 and 1940, Kiswahili was widely taught in Kenya both as a subject and as a medium of instruction. But after 1949 Kiswahili, the all-Kenya working-class and national language, 'was to be dropped out of all rural schools' (Mũtahi).

This oppression of Kenyan languages during colonial and post-colonial times went hand in hand with suppression of the cultures of the various nationalities. For instance, in Central Province the big *Itũĩka* cultural festival of dances, songs, and poems, and instrumental music was banned. Again during the same British colonial presence, the only poems and songs ever banned were those composed in Kenyan languages. Some well known examples were the *Mũthĩrĩgũ* dance and song in the 1930s, and the Mau Mau patriotic literature in the 1950s. Newspapers written in Kenyan languages and carrying pro-Kenyan patriotic news and news interpretation, like *Mũmenyereri* were banned. Books, like Jomo Kenyatta's *Kenya Bũrũri wa Ngũĩ*, written in Kenyan languages for the direct consumption by Kenyan peasants and workers, were banned. In other words, any and every progressive anti-imperialist literature, oral or written, in Kenyan languages has always been banned. It is a sad commentary in our post-independence cultural situation that following in the footsteps of the colonial practices as out-lined above, the only literature suppressed by our independent Kenyan government was the very first major modern theatrical effort in a Kenyan language. I am referring to the refusal by the Kenya government to licence the peasants and workers of Limuru to continue the public performance of *Ngaahika Ndeenda* by Ngũgĩ wa Thiong'o and Ngũgĩ wa Mĩrĩĩ at Kamĩrĩĩthũ Com-munity Education and Cultural Centre in November 1977, and the subsequent detention of one of the authors. Recently, July 1979, the girls at Riara Secondary School, Kiambu wrote and performed a play *Thĩ Ĩno Ĩhaana Atĩa Andũ Aitũ*, (*What a World*) in Gĩkũyũ depicting the plight of a plantation worker who has to live on 300 hundred shillings a month. The school was raided by the secret police and the teacher in charge was closely questioned. To the best of my knowledge, not a single book, poem, play, even the most racist and pro-imperialist, in English or any foreign language has ever been stopped in Kenya.

Today while the *comprador* ruling class in Kenya is busy suppressing Kenyan languages and patriotic Kenyan theatre in Kenyan languages, the foreign imperialist embassies have in-tensified their foreign languages programmes, their foreign language theatre programmes, and their foreign language cinema programmes, as well as providing Kenya, as part of their Techni-cal Aid Programmes, with 'free' language teachers to take charge of foreign language programmes in Kenyan schools and colleges. Even Brazil has 'donated' for 'free' a Brazilian professor to teach Brazilian Portuguese.

Thus in making their choice, Kenyan writers should remember not only the above historical, cultural struggle between the national and the foreign, but also the following words from Shabaan Roberts:

Na juu ya lugha, kitabu hiki changu husema katika shairi jingine kuwa titi la mama litamu lingawa la mbwa, lingine halishi tamu. Hii ni kweli tupu. Watu wasio na lugha ya asili, kadiri walivyo wastaarabu, cheo chao ni cha pili dunia — dunia ya cheo.[11]

And lastly in making their choices, Kenyan writers should

remember that no foreigners can ever develop our languages, our literatures, our theatre for us: that we in turn cannot develop our cultures and literatures through borrowed tongues and imitations.

Only by a return to the roots of our being in the languages and cultures and heroic histories of the Kenyan people can we rise up to the challenge of helping in the creation of a Kenyan patriotic national literature and culture that will be the envy of many foreigners and the pride of Kenyans. Titi la mama litamu lingawa la mbwa, lingine halishi tamu.

Notes

1. Speech read at the Kenya Press Club, Nairobi, on 17 July 1979.
2. Obi Wali, 'The Dead End of African Literature', *Transition*, 10, 1963.
3. Wole Soyinka, letter to the Editor, *Transition*, 11, 1963.
4. Ezekiel Mphahlele, letter to the Editor, *Transition*, 11, 1963.
5. ibid.
6. Ali Mazrui, *Cultural Engineering and Nation Building in East Africa*, (Evanston, Northwestern Press, 1972). See also his other books such as *The Anglo-African Commonwealth*, or *The African Condition* (London, Heinemann, 1980).
7. Taban lo Liyong, *The Last Word* (Nairobi: East African Publishing House, 1969). See particularly the opening essay, 'My Father'.
8. Gerald Moore, *The Chosen Tongue* (Harlow, Longman).
9. Marx and Engels, *The German Ideology*.
10. Taken from Mutahi's unpublished paper.
11. Shabaan Roberts, *Masomo Yenye Adili*, 1967, p. 103.

Postscript to Part I
On Civilization[1]

▲▲

Civilization, like so many words in common usage, is really a complex phenomenon with different meanings and connotations for different nations and classes. But broadly it refers to a state of bringing nature under human control. It is therefore not a uniform process identical for all people at all times.

In other words, civilization is not a static state. Different people have had different civilizations. Civilizations do rise and fall, do in fact change, even for the same nations and races.

There are two very important struggles in the life of man: the struggle with nature; and the struggle with other men for the control of the material produced from the struggle with nature.

When man lived completely at the mercy of nature (of which he is a part) he cannot be described as having been civilized. But when man joined hands with other men and started taming nature and in the process developed tools for the conquest of nature, he was making the first steps towards civilization. In other words, human labour, co-operative human labour that is, is basic to the process of civilization. In the process of conquering nature through co-operative labour, man also created a social environment, or a social nature. If man is not a slave to natural nature (or the natural environment) he is not civilized. But it is equally true that if a man is a slave to social nature (social environment) he cannot be said to be civilized.

We can now narrow down the concept. Civilization refers to recognizable historical high points or landmarks in man's struggle to bring both the natural order and social nature under human co-operative control.

Ngũgĩ wa Thiong'o in answer to a listener's question on BBC Africa programme, July 1979.

Seen in this light, there has not been as yet any truly human civilization. For instance, today America has reached hitherto undreamt of heights in the conquest of nature through a fantastic development of instruments of labour (i.e. technology). But America is today a man-eats-man society. In the realm of social nature, America is still in a state of social cannibalism. It eats its own children and the children of other lands especially of Africa, Latin America and Asia. What I have said of America is generally true of what has been called western civilization.

Some African civilizations had not developed the conquest of nature to a very high degree; but they had developed to a high degree their control of social nature.

No civilization has so far been built on the basis of blind imitation of other people. We, in Africa, do not have to imitate other people's languages, other people's mannerisms, other people's cultures, in order to be civilized. We must, in fact, build on our national languages and national cultures, and on our own co-operative labour.

Because no civilization has as yet been a truly complete human civilization, we must all strive for that human civilization which ensures adequate clothing, shelter and food for everyone; that civilization which ensures that all the benefits of modern science and the arts are available to everyone; that civilization which ensures the end of social cannibalism on earth.

In concrete terms this means a strenuous struggle against imperialism and its class allies in Africa, Latin America and Asia. To struggle against imperialism and its *comprador* allies is to struggle for a truly human civilization.

PART 2
Writers in Politics

6 Writers in Politics[1]

▲▲▲

> We cannot pose the problem of native culture without at the
> same time posing the problem of colonialism for all native
> cultures today are developing under the peculiar influence
> of the colonial, semi-colonial and para-colonial situations.
> *Aimé Césaire*

There is a dramatic poem of L. S. Senghor in which a white man
is so overwhelmed by Chaka's power and mastery over language
that he exclaims: 'my word Chaka . . . you are a poet . . . a
politician.'

The poet and the politician have certainly many things in
common. Both trade in words. Both are created by the same
reality of the world around us. Their activity and concern have
the same subject and object: human beings and human relationships. Imaginative literature in so far as it deals with human
relationships and attempts to influence a people's consciousness and politics, in so far as it deals with and is about operation
of power and relationship of power in society, are reflected in
one another, and can and do act on one another.

There is no area of our lives including the very boundaries of
our imagination which is not affected by the way that society is
organized, by the whole operation and machinery of power:
how and by whom that power has been achieved; which class
controls and maintains it; and the ends to which the power is
put. The class in power, for instance, controls not only the productive forces of the community — what is produced, how it is
produced and how it is shared out — but cultural development as
well. The means of life, and how they are produced, exchanged
and shared out and the social institutions that the whole process

gives rise to do move men, do profoundly affect the very quality
of their lives: how they eat, laugh, play, woo and even make
love. This universe — of moral significance of values and the
quality of human life — is what imaginative literature is about.
This universe is itself both a product and a reflection of the
material process of living. Literature and politics are about
living men, actual men and women and children, breathing,
eating, crying, laughing, creating, dying, growing, men in history
of which they are its products and makers.

The way power in society is organized can affect writers and
their writing in three ways:

1) The writer as a human being is himself a product of history,
of time and place. As a member of society, he belongs to a
certain class and he is inevitably a participant in the class
struggle of his times. As a writer in a given society, it does make
a difference whether he is allowed to write or not; whether
what he writes is controlled or not; and whether he is espousing
this or that class outlook.

2) A writer's subject matter is history: i.e. the process of man
acting on nature and changing it and in so doing acting on
and changing himself. The entire changing relations of production and hence the changing power relations consequent on
mutable modes of production is a whole territory of a writer's
literary concern. Politics is hence part and parcel of this literary
territory.

3) The product of a writer's imaginative involvement — what
Shakespeare called mirror unto nature — becomes a reflection
of society: its economic structure, its class formation, its conflicts and contradictions; its class power political and cultural
struggles; its structure of values — the conflict and tensions
arising from the antagonism between those which are dying and
those which are pointing to the future. Hence literature has
often given us more and sharper insights into the moving spirit
of an era than all the historical and political documents treating
the same moments in a society's development. The novel in
particular, especially in its critical realist tradition, is important in that respect: it pulls apart and it puts together; it is both
analytic and synthetic.

The relationship between the poet and politician, or between
writers and politics, is particularly important in our situation
where our cultures — our literature, music, songs, dances — are

developing under the strangulating embrace of western industrial and finance monopoly capital and the fierce struggles of
our people for breath even. The embrace of western imperialism
led by America's finance capitalism is total [economic, political,
cultural]: and of necessity our struggles against it must be
total. Literature and writers cannot be exempted from the
battlefield.

In Africa the relationship has taken various forms. Often the
writer and the politician have been the same person. In the very
process of articulating a people's collective consciousness, the
writer is led into active political struggles. Léopold Sédar Senghor
is a case in point. Or the politician steeped in active political
struggle takes up the pen as a necessary and a most important
adjunct to his involvement. Agostinho Neto[2] is an outstanding
poet and politician. For him the gun, the pen, and the platform
have served the same ends: the total liberation of Angola. But
whether actively involved in political struggle or not, many
African writers have often found that the very subject-matter
of their poems and stories has placed them on the wrong side
of the ruling cliques. Most South African writers — Dennis
Brutus, Ezekiel Mphahlele, Bloke Modisane, Alex la Guma,
Mazisi Kunene, Lewis Nkosi — are now in exile, while those
who remained, like Can Themba, were slowly strangled to death
by the racist atmosphere and system of violent repression. Their
books, need I say, have all been banned, and this is not surprising
in a nervous fascist outpost of western imperialism and monopoly capital that bans *Black Beauty*, the story of a horse, because
it might carry the implication of black being beautiful.

Even where the writer has not ordinarily been actively immersed in politics, i.e. in a situation where the writer does not
consciously see himself in terms of political activism either as an
individual citizen or in the subject matter of his literary concern,
he may well find himself suddenly involved in the hot political
power struggles of the day. Christopher Okigbo who once re-
marked that he wrote his poems for poets only and that anyway
he would rather have lived fully than write, died for the Biafran
secessionist cause. The others — Chinua Achebe, Gabriel Okara,
Cyprian Ekwensi — who in an earlier decade of optimism had
put African literature on the world map were all active in Biafran
politics. The involvement was what prompted Achebe to write
thus in 1969:

It is clear to me that an African creative writer who tries to
avoid the big social and political issues of the contemporary
Africa will end up being completely irrelevant like that
absurd man in the proverb who leaves his house burning to
pursue a rat fleeing from the flames.[3]

A very apt image that dismisses the case for non-involvement art
for art's sake approach to the writing of literature.

But while I agree with Chinua Achebe, there is a sense in
which no writer of imaginative literature from the very best to
the moderately significant can really avoid the big issues of the
day, for literature to the extent that it is a mirror unto man's
nature must reflect social reality or certain aspects of social
reality. How beautifully we get from Shakespeare, Marlowe,
Jonson, Rabelais a feel of sixteenth century English and French
societies: the emerging empirical spirit, the bourgeois individualism, the mercantile capitalist spirit struggling against feudalism
for the freedom to move and conquer the seas, to colonize and
christianize natives, crying in the same breath: my God, my
Gold; my Gold my God. Unforgettable too is the frenzy, the
trembling rage of the characters in nineteenth century Russian
fiction reflecting the volcanic rumblings of the peasants' and
the workers' struggle against tsarist feudalism and capitalism
that later ushered a new socialist order in the world. On the
other hand Jane Austen is often criticized and accused of in-
sulating herself from the big upheavals of her day — but even
she unwittingly gives a wonderful picture of a leisurely parasitic landed middle class in eighteenth century England. Or
Emily Brontë isolating herself in the Yorkshire moors, setting
her novel *Wuthering Heights* in the same moors, amidst the
local howling wind and rainstorms, but giving us a most incisive
examination of the limiting repressive and oppressive ethical
values of an industrial bourgeois class with all its suffocating
comforts derived from the exploitation of the working class
and the people of the colonies.

But Chinua Achebe is more right in the basic sense of relevance, concern and the commitment of literature to society.
What is important is not only the writer's honesty and faith-
fulness in capturing and reflecting the struggles around him, but
also his attitude to those big social and political issues. It is not
simply a matter of a writer's heroic stand as a social individual

— though this is crucial and significant — but the attitudes and the world view embodied in his work and with which he is persuading us to identify vis-à-vis the historical drama his community is undergoing. What we are talking about is whether or not a writer's imaginative leap to grasp reality is aimed at helping in the community's struggle for a certain quality of life free from all parasitic exploitative relations — the relevance of literature in our daily struggle for the right and security to bread, shelter, clothes and song, the right of a people to the products of their own sweat. The extent to which the writer can and will help in not only explaining the world but in changing it will depend on his appreciation of the classes and values that are struggling for a new order, a new society, a more human future, and which classes and values are hindering the birth of the new and the hopeful. And of course it depends on which side he is in these class struggles of his times.

There are however two types of writers defined by their attitudes to society. There are those who assume that a society is basically static and stable either because they live in a period when society is generally assumed to be stable or because cocooned in their class or being prisoners of the propaganda of the dominant class become insensitive to basic structural conflicts. English novelists like George Eliot in the nineteenth century tend to assume such a stability of the basic static structure. Her world is vast, the issues she is dealing with are wide, but the intellectual and moral conflicts do not arise out of an awareness of a changing world — a world consistently in motion, always in the process of transforming itself from one form to another, and hence giving rise to new class alignments and possibilities of new social orders. What interests such writers is just the moral conduct of their characters whatever their class, race or religious origins. Such writers have often an ideal of conduct or human type to which the different characters approximate with differing degrees of success and failure. At their best, these writers can and do produce a literature of sharp social criticism. But such an attitude to society, such an abstraction of human types and moral ideals from their basis in the class structure and class struggle, often gives rise to a literature distinguished for its shallow dive into society and only redeemed from oblivion by those of our critics who have no other critical tools apart from the worn and meaningless phrases like 'human compassion' 'timeless and universal' etc. Haven't we heard critics who demand of African writers that they stop writing about colonialism, race, colour, exploitation, and simply write about human beings? Such an attitude to society is often the basis of some European writers' mania for man without history — solitary and free — with unexplainable despair and anguish and death as the ultimate truth about the human condition.

But other writers, either because of the nature of the period in which they live, or because of their instinctive or conscious dialectical approach to life and society do not assume a static stability. The very conduct of their characters is firmly rooted in history and changing social conditions. [Being aware of a changing world, great writers like Aesychlus, Shakespeare, Tolstoy, Conrad, Sholokhov, Chinua Achebe, place conflicts between peoples in differing classes with their differing and often antagonistic conceptions of world order: of who holds, who should hold power, the ends toward which the power is put, and of the possibilities of a new social order from the womb of the old. The tragic dilemma of Okonkwo and Ezeulu is so profound and encompassing because at the basis of their conduct and decisions are two world orders in irreconcilable conflict: Okonkwo's world of emergent feudalism based on family and partly slave labour and that European colonial capitalism and imperialism based on racism and ruthless exploitation of African labour power by European capital. The old classes and social, economic and political order and its entire value structure is challenged by new classes and a new structure of values. In Joseph Conrad's novel *Nostromo* set in a fictional Latin American republic the issues are not the simplistic ones of a Christian morality and that of America's Wild West — absolute good (God) versus absolute evil (satan). Here in this Latin American republic where British and American mining interests hold power there is not universal-once-for-all-time ideals of conduct to which people conform or fail to conform. Here morality, religion, ethics are rooted in class: we can only adequately evaluate the characters' conduct and alienation by recognizing the historical, economic, class and racial basis of the conflicting moralities and outlooks. Here, as in Achebe's Nigeria, is no metaphysical evil versus metaphysical good. Imperialism and the exploitation of the labour power and the

natural resources of the colonized peoples by international
monopoly capital is at the root of the problems. Hence Conrad's
images of coal, ivory, silver that abound in his novels.

The African writer and Joseph Conrad share the same world
and that is why Conrad's world is so familiar. Both have lived
in a world dominated by imperialism. They have known Hola
camps, My Lai, Algiers, Sharpeville, the Arab mother and
child driven from Palestine. They have seen the bowels of
pregnant mothers ripped open; they have witnessed the artistic
finesse of the colonial mercenary hewing the bodies of struggling peasants and workers as carcasses fit for the God of
profit. They have seen the workings of justice in a social system
whose base is capitalism so well described by Shakespeare
in *King Lear*:

> . . . Plate sin with gold,
> And the strong lance of justice hurtless breaks;
> Arm it in rags, a pigmy's straw does pierce it.

They have witnessed mercenaries, coup d'états, and they know
that Macbeth's bloody dagger is not a figment of imagination
from heated brains of starry-eyed idealists. Have they not seen
imperialist dogs of war and oppression bathe in blood of the
people in neo-colonial regimes and crying out in glee:

> How many ages hence
> Shall this our lofty scene be acted over,
> In states unborn and accents yet unknown.

Theirs is a world in which societies are demonstrably changing
much of the time with the proletariat and the poor peasants
with a section of the petty bourgeoisie and the *lumpenproletariat*
struggling against a combination of local big business and
foreign business interests and against the political and cultural
system protecting the status quo. The economic, political and
cultural struggle between the various classes finds itself trans-
mitted into the writers' work. The situation, especially in the
colonial era, compelled many writers into a progressive ideological stance: they were swept off their feet as it were by the dy-
namic force and vision of a total national liberation. Hence much
of African literature was anti-colonialist and anti-imperialist:

Much of this writing then was against a background of hope
for better and more egalitarian black organized states. But like

Conrad whose bourgeois position limited his vision making him, for instance, unable to condemn British imperialism, the African writer's petty-bourgeois position could not allow him to see the nature of imperialism and the need for a continuous class struggle against it and its local *comprador* allies. I myself can remember writing in 1962 how I looked forward to the day when all the preoccupation of African writers with colonial problems and politics would be over and we would all sit back and poke sophisticated irony at one another and laugh at ourselves whatever that was supposed to mean: we would then indulge in the luxury of comedies of social manners (what a philistine hollow bourgeois ideal!) or explore the anguished world of lonely individuals abstracted from time and actual circumstances.

Often we never moved beyond blackness, beyond the racial aspect of the struggle for national liberation from colonial rule, to see what was basic to colonial oppression: the fact that we were part and parcel of a world-wide system of production called capitalism: the fact that the colonial, political and cultural invasion was to make conquest in the economic sphere more entrenched and permanent: and therefore that the African people's anti-colonial struggle was more than a racial struggle. It was also, and more fundamentally, a struggle against that system that for four hundred years had devastated a continent. It was Africa that fed capitalism from its beginnings in slavery, through the colonial phase to the current phase of neo-colonialism with all the intricate tubes leading from Africa to the metropolis of the western world.

Even today the African writer has often refused to see that values, cultures, politics and economics are all tied up together, that we cannot call for meaningful African values without joining in the struggle against all the classes that feed on a system that continues to distort those very values. We must join the proletarian and the poor peasant struggles against the parasitism of the *comprador* bourgeois, the landlords and chiefs, the big business African classes that at the same time act in unison and concert with foreign business interests.

The fundamental opposition in Africa today is between imperialism and capitalism on the one hand, and national liberation and socialism on the other: between a small class of native 'haves' which is tied to international monopoly capital and the masses of the people. Within that fundamental antagonistic contradiction is the opposition between the urban and the rural, between relatively highly developed pockets of the country and others close to the stone ages. The cut-throat competition between the emergent native bourgeoisie of the various nationalities who try to identify their interests as the interests of the whole ethnic group (nationality) can often blind us to these more real, more basic contradictions which link us to the class struggles in Asia, Latin America, Europe and America.

Faced with these contradictions, the African writer can often retreat into individualism, mysticism and formalism: such an African writer who often can see the shortcomings of the neo-colonial economies, the consequent distortion of values, the fascism in so many neo-colonial ruling classes, is at the same time scared of encountering socialism as an alternative social system. He is scared of the possibility of the working class and the peasantry controlling the productive forces and consequently of their seizure and exercise of political power as the only route to that control of the means of production. To avoid the two alternatives — the continuation of a neo-colonial status quo and the violent overturning of that status quo by the masses — he makes a cult of Africanness, of Blackism, of the dignity of the African past, of the African approach to problems; or he simply becomes cynical and laughs at everything equally; at capitalism and its exploitative and oppressive social system and at the struggles of the people for total liberation: or he may condemn every effort and everything — gains and losses in the struggle — in the name of abstract humanism, abstract universalism without seeing that free unfettered human intercourse is impossible within capitalistic structures and imperialism: that true humanism is not possible without the subjection of the economy, of the means of production (land, industries, the banks, etc.) to the total ownership and control by the people; that for as long as there are classes — classes defined by where or how the various people stand in relation to the means of production — a truly human contact in love, joy, laughter, creative fulfilment in labour, will never be possible. We can only talk meaningfully of class love, class joy, class marriage, class families, class culture.

What the African writer is called upon to do is not easy:

it demands of him that he recognize the global character of imperialism and the global character or dimension of the forces struggling against it to build a new world. He must reject, repudiate, and negate his roots in the native bourgeoisie and its spokesmen, and find his true creative links with the pan-African masses over the earth in alliance with all the socialisitic forces of the world. He must of course be very particular, very involved in a grain of sand, but must also see the world past, present, and future in that grain. He must write with the vibrations and tremors of the struggles of all the working people in Africa, America, Asia and Europe behind him. Yes, he must actively support and in his writing reflect the struggle of the African working class and its peasant class allies for the total liberation of their labour power. Yes, his work must show commitment, not to abstract notions of justice and peace, but the actual struggle of the African peoples to seize power and hence be in a position to control all the forces of production and hence lay the only correct basis for peace and justice.

In conclusion, I would like to single out one African writer who exemplifies the kind of commitment that I have been talking about. He is Sembene Ousmane, a Senegalese, and who gave us *God's Bits of Wood*. Read it — an account of the Senegalese workers' struggle in 1948 — and you'll see how he analyzes and then synthesizes; how he is involved in the particular without losing time, you feel that he is with the people, that it is their fate and their eventual triumph in which he is interested. He also wrote a poem called 'Fingers' and it illustrates the vision informing his work:

Fingers, skilful at sculpture
At modelling figures on marble,
At translation of thoughts
Fingers that would impress,
Fingers of artists.
Fingers, thick and heavy
That dig and plough the soil
And open it up for sowing,
And move us,
Fingers of land tillers.
A finger holding a trigger
An eye intent on a target finger.
Men at the very brink

Of their lives, at the mercy of their finger
The finger that destroys life.
The finger of a soldier.
Across the rivers and languages
Of Europe and Asia
Of China and Africa,
Of India and the Oceans,
Let us join our fingers to take away
All the power of their finger
Which keeps humanity in mourning.[4]

Unless we as African writers embrace such a vision — a vision anchored in the struggles of the people — we shall succumb to self-despair, cynicism, and individualism, or else we become mesmerized by superficial bourgeois progress which in the words of Karl Marx has never been possible without dragging individuals and peoples through blood and dirt, through misery and degradation. To borrow words from the same author, bourgeois progress resembles that hideous pagan idol who would not drink nectar but from the skulls of the slain.

The reign of that pagan idol in Africa is doomed. African writers must be with the people in burying the imperialist idol and his band of white and black angels, for ever.

Notes

1. Public lecture, given in the department of literature series in October 1975.
2. Now (1976) the President of the People's Republic of Angola.
3. Chinua Achebe, 'The African Writer and the Biafran Cause', *Morning Yet on Creation Day* (Heinemann, London, 1975), p. 78.
4. Sembene Ousmane, 'Fingers' quoted in *Lotus Awards 1971*, published by the Permanent Bureau of Afro-Asian Writers.

7 J. M. – A Writer's Tribute[1]

▲▲▲

I first heard of him in 1963. His book *Mau Mau Detainee* had
just come out. It was immediately the centre of a critical rage
and storm. The imperialist foreigners then in the offices of the
Nation Newspapers would not allow the African staff to review
it. They handled it themselves in order to smear the book and
its author and his celebration of Mau Mau resistance. The European bourgeois and the settler establishment in Kenya were
angry and bitter, not simply because Oxford University Press,
a pillar of the British literary publishing world, had brought out
a book on Mau Mau; not even because Margery Perham, a liberal
doyenne of the British academic establishment had written a
favourable foreword, but because an African, a Kenyan native,
had dared to write openly and proudly about Mau Mau as a
national liberation movement. They, together with the bourgeois
brainwashed African intellectuals who later reviewed the book
in academic journals, were stunned. They did not know how to
cope with Kariūki. How could they handle a Kenyan whom
they had not managed to cage and tame in the corridors of their
hollow colonial schools; a Kenyan who looked to his past and
to his involvement in Mau Mau, not with guilt, not with any
qualifying apologia, but with a positive glow of pride and
achievement; a Kenyan who could state that the Mau Mau oath
to liberate Kenya from sixty years of British imperialist robbery
of a people's soil and soul turned him into a man, a complete
man, restored to his humanity? Kariūki had refused to be defined
in a framework of values set by the oppressor and it was with a
contemptuous tone of triumph that he wrote of his enemies:
Lord forgive them for they know not what they are doing!

Later in 1964 I met him in his office in Nairobi, near the law
courts, the present site of the Kenyatta Conference Centre.

He was then not only the MP for Nyandarua North but also leader of the National Youth Service. I wanted to write an article on him, the first in a projected series on people's representatives (MPs) at work. I wanted him to give me a day when I could follow him touring his constituency. My novel, *Weep Not Child* had just been published and we talked about it. We also talked a little about his book *Mau Mau Detainee*. 'Aah, but all the money from it has gone into Income Tax,' he laughed, leaning back on the chair. The open laughter made me feel easy and relaxed. He told me that he was planning another book on political revolutionary movements in eastern Europe. He mentioned Yugoslavia and the people's resistance movement against the German occupation forces in the Second World War. I knew nothing about these struggles, but I went away thinking.

My colonial university education at Makerere had blinded me to the true nature of colonialism and imperialism. It had turned me into a parrot and an animated puppet mouthing out phrases prepared for me in European text-books. But Kariũki's education in the settled area, in the streets of political struggle with the masses, in the universities of Manyani and other concentration camps, had opened him out to see the link which bound the peasants and workers of Kenya to all others struggling against oppression and exploitation.

I never wrote the article, for I soon after resigned from the *Nation*. But throughout my studies and teaching in England, Kenya, Uganda, America and back in Kenya in 1972, I kept on following Kariũki's activities, speeches and writings with keen interest. For here was a writer and a critic raising issues which were troubling me as a writer: neo-colonialism, imperialism, the rise of an African ruling class of wealthy people, the insulted and humiliated majority of Kenyan people, the need and the necessity for unity among the peasants and workers from the ocean to the lake. I wanted to meet him again or hear him talk. But he was never allowed a political gathering. So when in 1973 I heard that he would speak at the United Kenya Club, I rushed there. He talked about many things from tourism, to the question of land, to the problem of Palestine. He kept his audience good-humoured and laughing with him. He had the pleasant touch of making an audience relax and be with him. I was not satisfied with one or two things he said about the Palestinian struggle and I waited for him outside the club. He

saw me: 'Oh, when did you come back from America?' I was
surprised that he could remember me, and more that he could
recall our encounter in 1964. 'You never came back,' he said.
I voiced my disagreement with his taking a neutral position between Israel's Zionist aggression and the Palestinian struggle. I
thought he should have come down firmly on the side of the
Palestinian struggle which was basically anti-colonial and anti-
imperialist. Israel and South Africa after all were in identical
positions as creations of western American imperialism. He said:
'Why don't you give me a ring so we can have time to discuss
this?' I somehow never went, though I kept on saying to myself
that there was always time. I would ask him about that book on
revolutions in Eastern Europe.

Today as I write this, I know I shall never have an answer
from his mouth. They are burying his body in Gilgil. But I
also know in a sense more deep than words can tell that on
Sunday, 2 March 1975, he wrote one of the most important
chapters in the Kenyan people's continuing struggle for a
meaningful national liberation from external and internal
exploitation and oppression and signed it with his blood.

Mau Mau Detainee was the earlier chapter in that national
quest for a social system in which no African child would go
hungry, go without adequate shelter, go without school, go
without a job — a system in which wealth and property and
the soil bought by the collective blood of the Kenyan people
would not end up in the pockets of a few Africans and Asians
and Europeans. It was as if in *Mau Mau Detainee* and in his
life he was posing the question: Why should the poor die, why
should women lose their husbands and sons and daughters only
to see Kenya's wealth, the product of their own sweat and
blood, go into the hands of a small class of exploiters?

On the Wednesday in 1975 when I learnt about his death, I
drove aimlessly round Limuru, then toward Nairobi, passing
through the tracts of tea and coffee plantations formerly owned
by British settlers but now owned by African individual landlords farming from their offices in the city. I looked at the
workers picking tea leaves, huge baskets on their plastic covered
bodies and I remembered that they were doing the same in the
1940s when I was a child. I reached my office to be confronted
by the bewildered faces at the University. So we shall never see
him again?

I recalled the betrayal of Lumumba, Mulele, Old Waiyaki, Kĩmathi, Achieng Oneko (who was never allowed to see his dying mother), of all the militants of early resistance movements against the British forces of occupation by the Nandi, Maasai, Gall, Akamba, Giriama, Luo, Gĩkũyũ and other Kenyan nationalities. Who betrayed J. M. Kariũki? Who killed him? I felt the truth pain, the truth hurt. For it was we, we who have kept silent and propped up an unjust oppressive system, because we were eating a bit of the fruits. So we kept quiet when Gama Pinto was killed; when Mboya was murdered; when Kũng'ũ Karumba disappeared. We kept quiet saying it was not really our *shauri*.

Then suddenly above the silence of my grief I heard students, youthful voices, shouting defiance, denouncing the lies, and singing poems to the struggle, voicing their determination to take up the fallen sword of J. M. and continue the struggle against inequalities in our land. British Imperialist Forces Out! they were shouting. I remembered that Mwangi is the name of a generation; and Kariũki means Born Again, or The Resurrected. Mwangi Kariũki. A generation resurrected. I remembered that encounter in 1964 when he was the leader of the National Youth Service and was talking of one Kenya, one people.

This generation will never keep silent again. Not even if they have to pay with their blood. That for me is the meaning and significance of Kariũki's death. A new generation was born on 2 March, on Ngong Hills, the heart of Maasai who for years kept away Portuguese, Arab and European invaders and destroyers from raping Kenya, our beautiful land. Never again shall we be humiliated, degraded, insulted, injured, laughed at in our homes in silence, for a new generation of socially conscious warriors was born again.

Notes

1. Weekly Review, No 7, 24 March 1975.

8 Born Again:
Mau Mau Unchained[1]

▲▲▲

Those of us who read *Mau Mau Detainee* when it first came out in 1963 admired the triumphant ring of hope rising above the sober and restrained tone of its rendering. We were equally unhappy about Margery Perham's liberal hesitancy and apologies in her lengthy introduction to the book. Why did she and her kind want to detain the Mau Mau resistance movement in a liberal prison?

It has been a painful experience to read again this account of the Kenya people's heroic struggle for a land in which, to use the author's words:

> Everyone will have an opportunity to educate himself to his fullest capabilities, in which no one will die or suffer through lack of medical facilities and in which every person will earn enough to eat for himself and his family.

Where have all our hopes gone? They have been replaced by a general feeling that water, water everywhere is bitter. For on 2 March 1975, Mwangi Kariũki was taken from a Nairobi hotel (it is rumoured that one of his captors had the uniform of the para-military GSU) to a valley in the Ngong Hills where he was shot dead after being beaten and tortured.

It is impossible not to see the parallel between this and a similar episode on 28 October 1953, when Kariũki had been taken from a Nakuru Hotel by an African police officer of the special branch and was whisked off to Kowop, a small detention camp in a valley between rocky hills near Lake Turkana to start on that forced journey which for seven years was to take him through fourteen concentration camps, often being beaten and tortured by the enemies of the Kenyan people.

There are other scenes which, again in retrospect, stand out stark and vivid in their prophetic symbolism. During his first detention in Manyani, the camp commandant was so incensed by Kariũki's exposure of the officer's cruel sadistic methods to a visiting committee that on the following day he took Kariũki to a place near the forest:

He said that he would shoot me unless I wrote down on a piece of paper that I would not send any more letters to England, that I would co-operate with the government and that I would help to type in the screeners' office. Although the thought of death was still not wholly desirable, I refused. He then took from his car a piece of three-ply wood about three feet by two feet and told me to hold it up above my head at arm's length. He walked five yards away and said that he was going to kill me if I did not agree to write the sentences. Still, not imagining he could be serious, I refused. To my horror he raised his gun and shot at me. I remember a tremendous noise and knowing that I was now dead and then nothing. He had, in fact, shot through the wood and I had fallen down with it. Out of the void I then heard the words '*Simama, simama*,' (Swahili for 'Get up'), and by a notable piece of deduction in the circumstances I decided that this was unlikely to be the language of heaven or hell and that I was therefore probably alive. As if hypnotized I stood up and faced him and we went through the rigmarole all over again. I refused and he shot again; again I fell into the abyss and emptiness and smelt death. Then distantly I heard '*Amka' amka*,' (Swahili for 'Wake up, wake up'), and the second time I rose from the dead. My body was now running with sweat and my mind was no longer able to grasp whereabouts we were or what was happening. 'For the third and last time,' he said, 'will you agree to write those sentences?' It was like a scene out of a film and without really knowing what I was being asked I repeated my 'No'. He fired again and this time I felt something sear through the base of the thumb on my right. Absolutely certain that I had at least been seriously wounded and was about to die I fell down again. When I saw the blood, which stained all my sweat so that wherever I felt was blood and still more blood, I rushed at him and clasped him round the waist and said, 'Look at this blood, you have killed me, there is blood all over me.'[2]

This can be seen as a preparation, a foretaste of the death he was going to die, and we can with confidence hope that he met his death with equal fortitude.

I have quoted the episode in full, not only because of the prophetic symbolic parallel with what was later to happen to him, not only too because it brings out Kariŭki's narrative technique — the matter-of-fact tone, the dead-pan humour, the piling up of details without over-dramatic decoration — but because it really shows the man that Kariŭki was: his total courage even in the face of death — his total uncompromising commitment to the people's political struggle against injustice, racism, and against economic inequalities and exploitation of the labour power of the masses, even if it meant paying for the commitment with his blood. It is an episode that brings out patriotism at its purest and most luminous.

The book is, for me, a profile in political courage, indestructible human will and determination; but it has other themes which are important in today's Kenya. I can only cite a few:

Education: Right from his youth, Kariŭki felt the need to arm himself with the weapon of literacy, with the power of reading and writing. But for Kariŭki education was meaningful only as a weapon in the service of the Kenyan people's anti-imperialist struggle. From the book, it is clear that he despised those Africans who saw their formal education, their ability to read and write, as setting them apart from the struggle of the people for the right to have adequate food, shelter and clothing in their own Kenya. Most of the educated in colonial schools became screeners, opportunists, collaborators with the enemy, all in exchange for the privileges and the safety of their own skins and stomachs. In contrast, Kariŭki and his other brothers, like Gad Kamau Gathumbi, seized every chance to share their knowledge of the alphabet with others. What can be more poignant than those literacy classes in Manyani, using smoothed and flattened earth as slates and sharp, pointed sticks as chalk and pen! Or more encouraging than the case of that old man of seventy-five, Kĩmana Wachuku, regularly attending Standard I classes to learn how to read and write and turn teaching them the history of Kenya he carried in his memories! Mutual education; mutual responsibility to one another; educators being educated; that (should have been) the guiding vision of our nation.

Unity of the Struggling Masses: Kariũki was concerned about the unity of the Kenyan people at the national level and of all the African people at the level of Pan-Africanism. Whichever camp he went to he tried to make friends with the people, learning their language and customs and local problems. What can be more illuminating of the spirit of Mau Mau detainees than the sharing of their meagre rations with the Turkana people? What a great sense of political discipline in the detainee's refusal to abuse or prostitute Kenyan womanhood, whether they were among the Akamba, the Luo or the Turkana? In the book, he wrote of Lodwar:

> We were shocked to see the terrible environment in which they struggled to live and we all felt that the government should give them more help even if it was at the expense of development in our own areas of Gĩkũyũ and Nyanza. We soon learnt some words in their language and began to give them food.[3]

Was the memory of this behind his personal involvement in, and contribution to all the collective efforts of our people all over Kenya? Of Pan-Africanism, he wrote:

> We are determined to press forward with the concept of an East African Federation, and move on to a union of East and Central Africa until we approach the great ideal of Pan-Africanists. None of us can rest quietly while any of our peoples, whether in Angola, Mozambique, South Africa, or Rhodesia is still under the imperialists' rule. There may yet be further sacrifices needed till they are free and we are ready to undergo them.[4]

Commitment to the Struggle: The Oath he took remained for him a commitment to the Kenyan people's struggle for their lands, for their total economic, political and cultural liberation. The commitment to a cause, to a group struggle, transformed him.

> My emotions during the ceremony had been a mixture of fear and elation. Afterwards in the maize I felt exalted with a new spirit of power and strength. All my previous life seemed empty and meaningless. Even my education, of which I was so proud, appeared trivial beside this splendid

and terrible force that had been given me. I had been born again and I sensed once more the feeling of opportunity and adventure that I had had on the first day my mother started teaching me to read and write. The other three in the maize were all silent and were clearly undergoing the same spiritual rebirth as myself.[5]

In the book he came back over and over again to this theme of the transforming power of the struggle with the masses. He for instance never considered escaping from prison since his place was with his fellow detainees. For him, those without formal schooling were the strongest in the struggle and he only wanted to put his brain power and skills at their disposal. He warned the leaders against betrayal of the masses, their faith, their love, their hope: 'Our leaders must realize that we have put them where they are, not to satisfy their ambition nor so that they can strut about in fine clothes and huge Cadillacs as ambassadors and ministers but to create a new Kenya.'[6]

Relationship with Kenyatta: Kariũki was first aroused to a political awareness by Kenyatta's voice in 1946. Although in the book, Kariũki emphatically denies Kenyatta's involvement in the Mau Mau Oaths ('I must, too, emphasize here that in all the statements and confessions made in my hearing by thousands of detainees in fourteen camps, the name of Kenyatta was never once mentioned as being involved in an oath'), he kept on reiterating his loyalty to him as the accepted head of the constitutional wing of the struggle. While in detention at Lodwar, Kariũki and others made a box and a hat which they sent to Kenyatta at Likitaung. When Kariũki was finally released, he sent Kenyatta supplies of Njahĩ 'as a mark of my deep respect for him'. He also sent him things in Maralal, 'some things he asked for to help him sustain his life in that place, and although I was not rich, I fulfilled every request to the utmost limit of my ability'. There is one revealing symbolic scene in the book describing Kariũki and his wife's visit to Kenyatta at Maralal where, after an exchange of gifts, they all sat down to eat.

When I had finished my plateful, Mzee asked if I would like some more. I replied that I had eaten enough. He then turned and said in the voice of a father: 'You are not in detention now. You and I must eat together until this food is finished.' I told him that I would agree as this was no time to start disobeying his roders. . . [7]

The Spirit of Resistance: It is this more than anything else that gives the book its enduring quality, as a prose of praise to an epic struggle. In the light of what has now happened, how can one forget the memorable comment about the beatings he got at Manyani:

I was stripped and given twelve strokes by a Mkamba sergeant. These were just about the most painful ones I ever received and they drew much blood from my buttocks. When the detainees saw my body, which was thin and bruised with the treatment we were receiving in Compound 6, they buzzed with anger like a swarm of bees. I was given strength to endure all these things because I knew that I was right and that all the other detainees thought I was doing right. This is the sort of strength that no amount of beatings can weaken. When will people realize that such beatings only stiffen the resolve of the victim? A beating may do some good when the person beaten knows he has done wrong, although I do not personally think so. But when he thinks that he has done right (whether he has or has not) beating immeasurably toughens his determination. Finally the authorities by their treatment were rapidly building me up as a martyr which was again contrary to their real objectives.[8]

One closes the book with a lot of soul-searching and self-questioning. I had just finished the book and I was thinking about the clandestine democratic organization in the detention camps (where democracy came from the people; where the rules were devised by the people at grass-roots); I was thinking about Kariũki's outspokenness which brought him so much personal suffering at the hands of all those who support colonialism, neo-colonialism and capitalism, when I got a poem sent to me anonymously through the post.

Whoever had sent it had scribbled a simple message, *Keep the faith*, and he or she had sent it because I had that very

week published an article in the *Weekly Review* as a writer's
tribute to *J. M.*

TO THE FACULTY

In Germany they first came for the communist
And I did not speak up because I wasn't a communist
Then they came for the Jew and
And I didn't speak up because I wasn't a Jew
Then they came for the trade unionists
And I didn't speak up because I wasn't a trade unionist
Then they came for the Catholics
And I didn't speak up because I was a Protestant
Then they came for me — and by that time no one was
left to speak up

Martin Niemoeller

The poem shows how fascism can divide a whole people on any
pretext so that they are eliminated one by one. The only correct
answer to fascism is resistance.

It is time that Kenyan intellectuals and all the progressive
youth, students, church-leaders, workers, took up Kariũki's call
and resolutely denounced and struggled against all the economic,
political and cultural forces that condemn our people to starvation wages, to landlessness, to lack of shelter, clothes and schools:
forces that have kept us only cultivating, planting, working, while
others reap and harvest and eat that which is a product of our
collective sweat, forces that are selling us to Euro-American and
Japanese imperialism.

Not to take up the call would mean that we too have joined
those who would detain the spirit of Mau Mau; only in such an
attempt we would merely be deceiving ourselves. For with
Kariũki's death, the spirit of Mau Mau, so well described in his
book, was set free and will no longer be chained to please the
British and other international imperialist interests. Mau Mau is
the spirit of all the Kenyan workers and peasants from Mombasa
to Kisumu. The day they shall join hands will make the earth
move, our earth, and linking hands with all the African peoples
on the continent and in the diaspora, they shall truthfully say:
Africa for the African people. This is the vision that guided
Kariũki, given expression in the *Song of Africa* that *J.M.* and
his fellow fighters composed on the occasion of Ghana's independence. The final verse goes:

Happy, happy, we shall be
When black people came together
To forge out unity
Universal Kingdom for all black people.[9]

Notes

1. A shortened version of this article appeared as a postscript to the 1975 re-issue of Mwangi Kariũki's, *Mau Mau Detainee*, (Nairobi, Oxford University Press, 1975).
2. Kariũki, op. cit., pp. 76—7.
3. ibid., p. 125.
4. ibid., p. 181.
5. ibid., p. 27.
6. ibid., p.181.
7. ibid., p. 179.
8. ibid., pp. 90—1.
9. ibid., p. 124.

9 Petals of Love[1]

▲▲

I would like to start by introducing to this audience the woman
who has all along inspired me, the woman who in fact made me
go to school to learn how to read and write. I am referring to
my mother, my peasant mother. I am happy that she is here tonight to witness the launching of *Petals of Blood* not only
because it is one of the results of my learning how to read and
write, but also because in so many ways the Kenyan peasantry
is the real actor in the novel. The turning of peasants into pro-
letarians by alienating them from the land, is one of the most
crucial social upheavals of the twentieth century, one moreover
fraught with pregnant possibilities for the future.

Now I really don't know what a writer is supposed to say on
an occasion like this because most writers are wordless when it
comes to speeches. Politicians are much better at that kind of
thing. We who use our pens are maybe writers in politics, but
we are not necessarily politicians. What anyway can writers say
about what they have already written? After all they have had
their say in between hard or soft covers.

For me, the *say* contained in between the hard and soft covers
of *Petals of Blood* took place over a period of six years, 1970 to
1975, with a spill over into 1976. It was a hard day's journey:
in the course of writing it, I would sometimes feel myself riding
on clouds of sheer excitement. But most were the times when I
felt totally fed up with the drudgery, the boredom, and the
frustrations of writing it: how did I ever come to be involved in
this madness of putting words together to form stories? How
did I ever get caught in this indulgence of fiction?

At such times I would remember those days in my peasant
mother's house where people often gathered to tell stories and
to compete in unravelling word riddles. I would go back to my

days in Maanguuũ and Kĩnyogoori Primary Schools where one teacher, Mr Samuel Kĩbicho, (now Dr Kĩbicho) insisted on my reading several story books such as Stevenson's *Treasure Island*, Dickens's *Oliver Twist* and other European classics in the Simplified English Series. My search for the origins of 'this madness' would take me to Alliance High School where I read more novels like Emily Brontë's *Wuthering Heights* and Tolstoy's *Childhood, Boyhood and Youth*; and then on to Makerere University College where on top of European literature, I was to discover the great wealth of African and West Indian literatures.

The headmaster of Alliance High School had said that Economics was that terrible subject which only Americans studied, certainly not a subject fit for sober English gentlemen. Well, I did not want to be a sober or an unsober English gentleman, hence I studied Economics. In preparing myself for the great task of NOT becoming any sober or unsober English gentleman, I had read a small book called *Teach Yourself Economics* or *Economics Made Easy*, in which the whole world capitalism was explained in terms of supply and demand and maximization of satisfaction under conditions of perfect competition in a free market, although it was a little different from the unfree market at Limuru where my mother used to buy us sugar-canes and ripe bananas. Of course the book, did not call this free market economy, *capitalism*: it was assumed that this was an eternal universal economic system and what was being studied was simply the objective laws governing its operation.

Then came a young lecturer — he was I think the only Kenyan or the only student then who had ever got a first class B.A. at Makerere — and who had gone on to the London School of Economics and performed as brilliantly. His name was Mwai Kĩbakĩ. What was very amazing that he was so brilliant and yet he did not have a Christian name! Anyway he talked to us about conditions of imperfect competition and he drew complicated graphs on the blackboard and he said that perfect competition was all fiction. He gave us a question on this imperfect competition and I scored very low, so I gave up economics. I preferred fiction to facts. I went on to study English Literature and Mr Mwai Kĩbakĩ left Makerere for the KANU headquarters in Nairobi where he became the party's Executive Officer. I feel honoured by his presence; the presence of my mother, my brothers, my wife Nyambura; and all your presence tonight.

Now my pursuit of literature, which I then thought was fiction, has brought me full circle to the facts of economics, that is to matters of what we produce and how, what we eat, what we wear, and what we shelter under: who controls what we eat, wear and shelter under? Economics is really the system of production, control and distribution of wealth and this ultimately determines every other aspect of life for, as Engels once said: 'mankind must first of all eat, drink, have shelter and clothing, before it can pursue politics, science, arts, religion.' How the wealth of our country is produced, who controls it, and how it is distributed should then be a matter for all our concern for it does affect us wherever we may be: in the library, in the church, or at the bar.

Literature, as part of culture, is really a reflection of the material reality under which we live. In trying to understand the distortion of Kenyan culture by imperialism, I have come to realise that no people can develop a meaningful national culture under any form of foreign economic domination. A people's total control of all their natural and human resources, their control of all the products of their labour, is truly the only condition for the flowering of a patriotic national culture. It is equally true that when a people's culture is dominated by foreigners, those people will be looking at and evaluating their material reality, their economic reality, through the distorted eye-glasses of those foreigners. They will be evaluating their history, their past and present achievements, their future potential, from the standpoint of imperialist foreigners who cannot possibly be wishing those people any unfettered prosperity and development. No country, no people can be truly independent for as long as their economy and culture are dominated by foreigners!

I was therefore horrified when, in the course of writing the novels, I came to realise that Kenya was poor, not because of anything internal, but because the wealth produced by Kenyans ended in developing the western world. It is simple. For every one unit of invested wealth from West Germany, France, Britain, Japan and America, the imperialist bourgeoisie takes away ten units of wealth back to those countries. Their aid, loans and investment capital that they gloat about are simply a chemical catalyst that sets in motion the whole process of expropriation of Kenya's wealth, with, of course, a few left-overs for the 'lucky' few. Imperialism, I came to realise, can never develop a country or a people.

This was what I was trying to show in *Petals of Blood*: that imperialism can never develop our country or develop us, Kenyans. In doing so, I was only trying to be faithful to what Kenyan workers and peasants have always realised as shown by their historical struggles since 1895. This history has often been distorted in our bourgeois schools, in our bourgeois universities, in our libraries often filled with the filthy results of bourgeois scholarship. But if the peasants and workers were to write in ink the history they have already written in blood and sweat, their standpoint would be closer to that of the worker looking at history in the poem by Brecht:

Who built the seven gates of Thebes?
The books are filled with the names of kings.
Was it kings who hauled the craggy blocks of stone?
And Babylon, so many times destroyed,
Who built the city up each time? In which of Lima's houses,
That city glittering with gold, lived those who built it?
In the evening when the Chinese wall was finished
Where did the masons go? Imperial Rome
Is full of arcs of triumph. Who reared them? Over whom
Did the Ceasars triumph? Byzantium lives in song,
Were all her dwellings palaces? And even in Atlantis
   of the legends
The night the sea rushed in,
The drowning men still bellowed for their slaves.

Young Alexander conquered India.
He alone?
Ceasar beat the Gauls.
Was there not even a cook in his army?
Philip of Spain wept as his fleet
Was sunk and destroyed. Were there no other tears?
Frederick the Great triumphed in the Seven Years War. Who
Triumphed with him?

Each page a victory,
At whose expense the victory ball?
Every ten years a great man,
Who paid the piper?

So many particulars,
So many questions.[2]

I am not as a Kenyan ashamed of speaking and writing about
the peasants and workers who have built Kenya and who,
through their blood and sweat, have written a history of
grandeur and dignity and fearless resistance to foreign economic,
political and cultural domination, a history of which we should
be proud.

If *Petals of Blood* can convey at least that message to us
Kenyan readers, I shall be satisfied. Hopefully out of *Petals of
Blood* we might gather petals of revolutionary love.

Notes

1. Speech at the formal launching of Ngugi's novel, *Petals of Blood*, in
   Nairobi in July 1977.
2. B. Brecht, 'Questions from a worker who reads' in *Poems 1929–1938*,
   edited by Willett and Manheim (London, Methuen, 1976), p. 252.

PART 3
Against Political Repression

10 The Links that Bind Us[1]

My wife and I are overwhelmed by the warmth with which we have been received by the people of Alma-Ata, this famed father of luscious apples, in the heart of Kazakhstan. Even the weather has been smiling: the sunshine on green trees and grass along the wide spacious city avenues; and of course the snow on Tien Shan mountains which, I am told, once formed a veritable fortress for those Kazakhs fighting against the foreign dictatorship of Ghengis Khan and other invaders in earlier times; and later, in the nineteenth century against Tsarist feudalism and oppression. I hope that all of you will visit Kenya and enjoy a similar sunshine in a land of green leaves and many-a-coloured flower and also the snow on Mount Kenya which, with the Nyandarwa Mountain ridges, was a refuge for those Kenyan patriots struggling against British imperialism.

I feel touched that my small efforts to sing about those patriots and their epic struggle have been honoured by this movement of African and Asian writers in the form of the Lotus Award. I feel proud to be in the company of such distinguished previous winners as Alex la Guma, Marcellino Dos Santos, Hiroshi Noma, Sonomyn Udval, Sembene Ousmane, Agostinho Neto, and others. I take this, not so much as a personal honour, but as a tribute to the creative efforts of writers in East Africa.

But equally important, especially in connection with the aims of this movement, the award to the songs that we have sung is a recognition of the basic and enduring links which bind the peoples of Africa and Asia and it is only appropriate that this year's prize is being given simultaneously to Kateb Yacine from Algeria, and Thu Bon from South Vietnam.

Friends, I will now seek your indulgence and patience and

for a few minutes echo the thoughts and words of the great genius of Pan-Africanism, W.E.B. Du Bois, by posing the question he once raised, though in a slightly differing context in his book *Dusk of Dawn*: What are the links that bind us?

The ties of geography are easier to see. Africa and Asia, two great continents, shake hands across the Suez Canal. The Indian Ocean anyway has never been a barrier and for centuries East Africa peacefully traded with China, India and Arabia before the arrival of the Portuguese who turned this creative trade into a traffic of destroyed cities, cultures and human beings for a little silver to fatten the coffers of bourgeois Europe.

This is an African story: it is also an Asian story and any cursory glance at the history of China, Indo-China, India, Africa, the West Indies and Afro-America, will see the testimony in tears and blood. We are truly a colonial people whose sweat has been cruelly exploited by western-monopoly capital to build the monument called western civilization. We groaned while they ate: our skins were caked dry in the mines and plantations while they drank water in the shade. We built their cities for them and ourselves slept in the gutter. They scattered us all over the globe and then added insult to injury by coming to our own homes and using their superior technology, itself built on black cargo across the middle passage, gunned us out and said the home was theirs.

Let me for a few minutes confine myself to Kenya. Here the missionary, the settler and the colonial governor came as three imperial massives of western monopoly-capital. The settler grabbed the land and exploited African labour. The governor protected him with political oppression of Kenyans and with the gun. And the missionary stood guarding the door as a colonial spiritual policeman. As Kenyan people were taken to work on tea and coffee plantations for the settler or conscripted to fight in European imperialist wars, the missionary had the audacity to tell them to lift up their eyes unto the Lord and sing alleluia — Aaamen!

In their racist books and in their colonial and bourgeois schools were the poetic and intellectual exultation of our humiliation and degradation. The best minds of Europe, Hume, Carlyle, Gustav Lebon, Froude, Hegel abetted in these cultural falsehoods. They sang of us as a people without history, and without meaningful values. This was drummed into our heads through their racist literatures and colonial schools: Europe was the centre; the universe revolved around Europe, the fountainhead of universal values and civilization.

In the name of that civilization, they destroyed our dances, our languages, our songs, our poetry. This was *not* a case of wanton carelessness; it was calculated. Literature, songs, dances and stories embody the image people have of themselves and of their place in the universe as they struggle to harness the energies of nature for their use. Colonialism then systematically tried to kill the African individual and collective image of self. Get at their self-hood, fervently urged the governor and the settler: the spiritual policeman wearing the cloak of a priest or that of a man of letters went about his task sometimes with the subtleness of a serpent, often with the awkward crudeness of the one-eyed giant. They told their African converts to sing: 'Wash me Redeemer and I shall be whiter than snow'. They all knew that a slave was not a slave until he accepted that he was a slave. So economic exploitation and political repression were accompanied by racist ideology for spiritual repression. This made a few of our westernized bourgeoisie cry in the words of Okot p'Bitek in his *Song of Ocol*: 'Mother, mother, why was I born black?'

But this gloomy picture is only one side of the story. A system of exploitation also gives rise to those forces which set out to destroy that system and its dire consequences. From our midst, from the midst of the people, arise new Prometheuses who wrest fire from the gods and light the path of liberation. So again in Kenya, right from the moment the settlers, the governor, and the missionary set foot in our land, people resisted: they fought back with sticks and spears and clubs, and guns and bare hands. They were often beaten: but they retreated only to reorganize and strike back. They were often defeated and the settler went to play polo, golf, tennis, and gymkhana, his fears assuaged: but this was only temporary — for the people came back even stronger, arming themselves with better weapons and a firmer unity arising from their consciousness of their common lot as peasants and workers, of their common link as an African working people.

On the cultural level, they refused to sing to the Lord asking to be washed white: they created their own songs, their own poetry, their own dances, their own literature. Often these songs and dances created by the people for the people in their economic and political struggle were banned by the colonial administration. But no amount of gunpowder can put down the creative spirit of a people. They composed new songs, invented new dances, even as they sharpened their swords and spears and cleaned their home-made guns or those wrested from the enemy. Behind them were the epic stories of Waiyaki-led heroic struggles against the British forces of occupation, of Koitalel's ten-year guerrilla warfare against the British; of Thuku's mass demonstration in the twenties. Later Kenyatta's book *Facing Mount Kenya* was to indicate the only way people could drive out the gentleman of the European jungle from their home: by meeting reactionary violence with revolutionary violence.

Came the greatest moment in our history when the Kenyan peasants and urban workers rose in armed struggle. They went to the mountains and forests and for eight years resisted the British military might. And still they sang:

We shall never stop fighting
For Kenya is an African people's country

They were re-enacting the scenes earlier acted out by their brothers both in Africa and in the western world. Nat Turner, Toussaint L'Ouverture, Dedan Kĩmathi: their full story and what they stood for has never really been told.

This is the story that East African writers, and indeed all African writers in their different ways, have been trying to tell. It is simple. The true literature of the African peoples, from the Americas and the West Indies to the continent of Africa, is written with the blood of the people on their black flesh. It is the literature of struggle: the struggle of ordinary people, who against great odds have nevertheless changed and are continuing to change oppressive social systems and hence the power map of the twentieth century.

In this, the progressive African writer has no choice other than of aligning himself with the revolutionary forces of change at every historical phase of the struggle. This has not been an easy task. It calls upon him to go beyond clichés and slogans. It calls upon him not only to capture the vibrations of the very intricate human interactions in space, but also their vibration and contradictions in the structural reformation of society in time. But whatever the difficulties, whatever the challenges to his craftsmanship and artistry, I have no doubt as I stand before this gathering that for the African writer his role is to be one with the people so as to articulate their deepest aspirations for freedom and a higher quality of life. This holds true for the writer in Asia, indeed all progressive writers from the oppressed world.

A shared experience of the past, a shared hope for the future: these then are the most enduring links that bind the African peoples on the continent and in diaspora with those of Asia. They are the links that bind us to the words of Abay Kunanbayav, the Kazakh poet of the nineteenth century, in his anguished cry:

Oh that freedom should reign
And that men could maintain
Conditions to favour, the clear, searching brain![2]

The links that bind us to the words of the Senegalese writer, Sembene Ousmane, in his poem against the one finger (the minority classes and imperialism) that holds the trigger of a gun aimed at the lives of the people:

Across the rivers and languages
Of Europe and Asia
Of China and Africa
Of India and the Oceans
Let us join fingers to take away
All the power of their finger
Which keeps humanity in mourning.[2]

Or to those of the Vietnamese poet Thu Bon in his celebratory certainty of victory:

Our hatred is the plough-share that plunges
    into the earth
One day it will re-erupt to the surface
On that day, my hand will make a chain with
    thousands of other hands
And we will emerge from the earth and go
    towards the azure.
Our guns will chastize the enemy
In order to bury him for ever into the depths
    of this earth.[3]

The links are enduring because as we struggle against the forces which exploit us, oppress us, humiliate us in South Africa, Mozambique, Angola, Rhodesia, Vietnam, Cambodia and Palestine, we are truly waging war against all those forces that exploit, oppress, humiliate and dwarf the creative spirit of man.

So why not now dream the hopes of millions: of a United People's Republic of Africa joining hands with a United People's Republic of Asia in the service of the true Republic of man and works. What greater story can we as writers be privileged to tell? We can only hope that our hearts and pens will always be equal to the task.

Notes

1. Acceptance speech of the Lotus prize in literature during the meeting of African and Asian Writers in Alma-Ata, Kazakhstan, 6 September 1973.
2. Sembene Ousmane, 'Fingers', quoted in Lotus Awards 1972, published by the Permanent Bureau of Afro-Asian Writers.
3. Thu Bon, 'My Underground', quoted in Lotus Awards 1973, pp. 17–18.

11 Repression in South Korea[1]

▲▲

News of the recent jailing of Kim Dae Jung and other leaders of the democratic movement in South Korea was received with shock by all the participants in the Emergency International Conference on Korea held in Tokyo, Japan, on 12–14 August.

One of the main resolutions of the conference was a call for the immediate release of all the civic leaders, students, religious people, writers, university teachers, and countless other political prisoners now rotting in the 'tiger cages' of the South Korean military dictator Park Chung Hee. The conference also called for the removal of 42,000 U.S. troops and nuclear personnel in South Korea and expressed its complete support for the movement for democratic rights and freedoms of speech, association, assembly, religion and for the peaceful reunification of Korea.

The conference, which was convened by the National Congress for Democracy and Unification of Korea with the help of a group of concerned Japanese writers led by Oda Makota, a novelist, was attended by prominent scholars and writers from Algeria, Australia, Canada, England, France, Hong Kong, Malaysia, Mexico, Singapore, South Korea, Sri Lanka, Thailand, U.S.A., and West Germany. These included such notables as George Wald, Harvard Professor and Nobel prize-winner in Biology. The conference had also the support of, among many others, Isio Askada (mayor of Yokohama City), Joan Baez (singer), Norman Mailer (novelist), and Noam Chomsky (linguist).

I was the only writer from East Africa and for me it was an eye-opener. I had read about the 4 July 1972 joint communiqué, simultaneously announced in Seoul and Pyongyang, which set out the three principles of North and South reunification: viz.,

Koreans, not foreigners, would take the initiative, would resort to peaceful means, and unity would transcend differences in the social systems. I had read about the subsequent declaration of martial law in South Korea on 17 October 1972 and Park's cynical comment that he would never entrust the fate of South Korea to a piece of paper and that unity would not be achieved within a hundred years. I had heard about the imprisonment of Kim Chi Ha, a Catholic poet and surely one of the leading writers in the world today. His crime was simply writing poems which Park did not like, but which were nevertheless enormously popular with the people. In these poems, now translated into English and published under the title, *Cry of the People*, we can hear the collective anguish of the South Korean people as well as their collective determination to be free. I had read about the abduction of Kim Dae Jung from a hotel in Japan by the dreaded Korean C.I.A. in 1973. His crime? That he had almost defeated Park in presidential elections despite intimidation and rigging of votes. I had also known about the 42,000 American military and nuclear personnel that prop up an otherwise tottering unpopular regime *à la* South Vietnam!

What I had not known was the extent of the internal repression and the cruel disregard for South Korean lives that makes the Park regime one of the cruellest in the world, perhaps only equalled by South Africa. It is a police state thriving on anti-Communist phobia, which it carefully nurses, and on the support of American troops. I had also not fully realised the massive strength of the movement for democratic restoration — it cuts across a wide spectrum of different shades of liberal persuasions — and the depth of their passionate commitment to reunification of South and North. I had to hear it from South Koreans of all ages and of different ideological shades and to see the pain and the seriousness in their faces and gestures. I can now understand the broad-based unity and the passions behind it.

Park seized power in 1961 with a *coup* that ended the liberal regime of the democratically elected prime minister, Chang Myon, who had taken office after the fall of the Syngman Rhee repressive regime in 1960. This means that except for a brief period following the liberation of Korea from years of Japanese colonialism in 1945, South Korea has never known peace, democracy and freedom. Park based his claim to power on his proclaimed need to build a strong government to counter an imagined possible attack from the People's Republic in North Korea. He immediately took several measures to kill all opposition to himself. The National Security Act was passed to outlaw conspiracy, instigation and propaganda in support of any presumed anti-state organisations. The Anti-Communist Law was also enacted to punish heavily any organisation assumed or suspected of working along any lines the regime thought were communistic, or to punish any person suspected of luring others into such an organisation, or suspected of praising it, encouraging it, or in any way benefiting it.

Under these two laws most liberals, writers and religious leaders who criticised the corruption, nepotism, unemployment, low salaries, and the living conditions of the people, were silenced by prison and detention. But this already tight control was further strengthened by the proclamation of the so-called Revitalisation (*Yushin*) Constitution of 1972. Article 53 of this fundamental law gave Park the right to take on emergency powers and hence to rule by decrees. Emergency Decree No. 1, declared on 8 January 1974, prohibited the denial, criticism or defamation of the *Yushin* Constitution. Decree No. 2 of the same date established an emergency court martial to try any crime against the emergency decrees. Decree No. 9, of 13 May 1975, forbade rumour-mongering, opposition to the constitution, meetings by students, and any criticism of the emergency decrees; the government, or rather Park, had full powers to expel offenders from school, places of work, and to ban publications. The criminal code was also revised, introducing crimes of slander against the state by South Koreans whether in or outside South Korea. Under this section, many Koreans have been abducted from Europe and Japan by the KCIA, which like its American counterpart, has a worldwide network.

These state terrorist activities of the Park regime against the South Korean people and their democratic and human rights are well illustrated in Kim Chi Ha's satiric poem, 'Groundless Rumours':

A timid peasant, An-Do, goes to Seoul to look for a job. On the verge of starvation after turning to every corner without any success in this supposedly modern prosperous city, An-Do stands on his own two feet, and for the first time in his life, protests against the world: 'What a bitch this world is!'

An-Do is heard by Park's secret police who hurl him to court

charging him with the crime of rumour-mongering against
the state. Let me quote from the poem:

No sooner had the words left his mouth than
Handcuffs were put on An-Do's hands and he was
    dragged to court.
Pounding his gavel three times,
The judge opened the hearing.
'What's the charge?'
'His crime is that of standing on his own two feet
    and spreading groundless rumours, Sir.'
'Aah, that is a big crime indeed.'
'The accused, by standing on the ground with
    his two feet and spreading groundless rumours,
    committed the crime of touching the ground
    with his two feet, the crime of resting his
    body, the crime of tranquillizing his mind, the
    crime of attempting to stand up despite his
    poverty-stricken status, the crime of wasting
    time in thinking, the crime of looking up
    at the sky without a feeling of shame, the
    crime of
Inhaling the air and expanding his thorax, the
    crime of forgetting his status and standing
    upright, which is granted only to the special
    privileged class, the crime of insolently
    avoiding the national policies for more
    production, export, and construction without
    a moment's rest, the crime of violating the
    3 'un's', 5 'no's', 7 'anti's', 9 'non's', the
    crime of
Thinking up groundless rumours which would
    mislead innocent people, the crime of
    intending to voice the same rumours, the crime
    of voicing the same, the crime of intending
    to spread the same, the crime of spreading
    the same, the crime of disrespecting the
    fatherland, the crime of disgracing his native
    language, the crime of comparing the
    fatherland to an animal, the crime of creating
    a possibility for the world to look on the

    fatherland as an animal, the crime of
Disturbing the environment for capital investment,
    the crime of promoting social disorder and
    creating social unrest, the crime of agitating
    the mind of the people, the crime of growing
    weary of life, the crime of escaping from
    existing customs, the crime of
Possibly helping the enemy, the crime of
    entertaining anti-establishment thought, the
    crime of possibly organizing an
    anti-government body through telepathic
    means, the crime of anti-government riot
    conspiracy, the crime of strong mindedness,
    and on top of it the crime of violating the
    special society manipulating law.'
'GUILTY.' the judge declared,
Pounding his gavel three more times.
'And it is hereby solemnly declared in
    accordance with the Law
That from the body of the accused shall be cut
    off immediately, after the closing of this court,
One head, so that he may not be able to think
    up or spread groundless rumours any more,
Two legs, so that he may not insolently stand on
    the ground on his two feet any more,
One penis and two testicles, so that he may not
    produce another, seditious like himself.
And after this is done, since there exists a great
    danger of his attempting to
Resist, his two hands shall be tied together behind
    his back, his trunk shall be
Tied with a wet leather vest, and his throat shall
    be stuffed with a hard and long-lasting
    voice-preventing tool, and then he shall be
    placed in confinement
For five hundred years from this date.'

'No!' he cries out.
Snip.
'No, my penis is gone!' Snip snap.
'My testicles too, no, no.' Crack.

'My neck, oh my neck is gone.' Hack hack.
'No, my two legs also gone.' Handcuffs, leather
    vest, voice-preventing tool.
So they brutally shoved the fellow An-Do
    into a solitary cell.

Not surprisingly the opposition to the *Yushin* Constitution —
surely a legalisation of brutal repression and oppression *à la*
South Africa — has united the various anti-Park forces on a
broad democratic front, from civic to religious leaders. The
church has been at the forefront of this struggle and many of its
leaders are now in prison. The democratic movement has received
support from many corners of the world and especially from in-
side the U.S.A. On 2 April 1976, a letter signed by about one
hundred and twenty prominent U.S.A. leaders, among them
Edward Kennedy, Walter F. Mondale, Frank Church and George
McGovern, was sent to President Ford. The letter expressed
distress at the continuation of suppression of South Koreans
who:

> . . . urge progress toward the restoration of democracy in
> their country. Several religious, academic and political
> leaders have been arrested and are being charged with plot-
> ting to overthrow the government after signing a declaration
> presented at a church service. . . . The policies of Park to-
> ward political dissidents not only violate internationally
> recognised standards of human rights but also raise serious
> questions about the supportive role of the United States in
> its relation with the Republic of Korea. . . .

The same issues were raised by Edward Kennedy in a senate
debate of 24 March 1976, when he stated, among other things:
'Yet what could be more fundamental to the principles of
democracy — and human rights — than freedom to criticise
one's own government?'
The Washington Post of 19 March 1976, described Park as:

> a dangerous man . . . on the loose in South Korea, one who
> threatens to provoke internal unheaval and to cost his
> country the support of its leading foreign ally. Indeed,
> given the ruthless centralisation of power in Seoul, this

man is in a position to do more damage to Korea's stability and security than any other figure.

But the main struggle is led by the South Koreans themselves under the umbrella of the National Congress for Democracy and Unification. I shall long remember the moving testimony of Professor Yun I Sang, an internationally recognised Korean composer, telling us how he was abducted from West Germany and taken to prison in Seoul where he was tortured. I shall long remember the letter from Kim Chi Ha talking to us so intimately about friendship although he was himself in prison:

> I think that of all the words that I love most dearly such as liberation, revolution, etc., the most brilliant is the word friendship by which you and I were forcibly bound together. Our aim must be to give an expansion, an historical expansion.

I shall long be haunted by the beautiful face and the soft voice of twenty-one year old Miss Yun Jong Hee telling us how she had never seen her homeland and how she could not now go home because as an active worker for the movement for democracy and reunification she would only be welcomed into prison . . . or the smiling face of twenty-year old Miss Lee Miyon telling me that she would never marry until South Korea was liberated.

The Emergency International Conference was hopefully the beginning of a concerted international pressure for democratic rights in South Korea, so that youngsters like Miss Yun Jong and Miss Lee and the 650,000 South Koreans exiled in Japan can return and help in rebuilding their motherland in unity and peace. This international pressure is often blunted by Park's orchestrated propaganda machine, which often buys whole pages in the western press to put across fabrications dressed as truth.

But the pressure seems to be mounting. What the South Korean people are asking for is simple. They want an end to internal repression and murder; an end to foreign domination; the withdrawal of all foreign troops and nuclear weaponry; and for the reunion with the fifteen million brothers and sisters in the north. It is true that Japan and the U.S.A. fear the united power of fifty-five million free Koreans, for South Korea where strikes are banned, is still one of the most lucrative areas for Japanese and American investments because of cheap labour.

The beneficiaries of the oppression of South Korean people are in fact the imperialist bourgeoisie of Japan and the U.S.A. and of course the South Korean comprador bourgeoisie whom Kim Chi Ha, calls the 'Five Bandits' in a poem of the same title. The Five Bandits (business tycoons; top bureaucrats; national assemblymen; the top military brass; cabinet ministers) who comprise the native ruling class headed by Park Chung Hee have one national anthem, one motto, one prayer:

Let's construct a bridge across the Strait of Korea with the bones of those who have starved to death, so we can worship the god of Japan! Like slave-masters of olden times, they drive the people to work harder and longer, with the beating of bursted drums and the sounds of broken trumpets, with one aim in mind: to increase their own wealth.

The lifestyle of the Five Bandits is the same:

They buy a Mercedes in addition to their black Sedans, but feign humility by riding in a Corona. They make their fortune by cheating the budget and further fatten it by illegal biddings, but chew gum to rid themselves of the smell of corruption. They shout loudly not to deal in foreign goods, while lighting up a Kent. They hastily write decrees to ban foreign goods and are pleased with how nicely the law was written. They deny their dishonesty to an 'ignorant' journalist who, hearing of a big scandal, rushes upon the scene. And for an answer they smugly whisper: 'What is your golf handicap?'

In this respect South Korea is like most Third World countries, although Park's propaganda portrays South Korea as part of the developed world — hence his promises of aid the country can hardly afford to some Third World countries. Anyway whatever the odds, those Koreans seem determined to continue their struggle.

'We shall return to a united motherland,' Yun Chung Ho of the South Korean Youth League told me. He quoted a few lines from Kim Chi Ha's poem 'Cry of the People':

Spring has come — the earth is waiting.
Now is the time to rise!

The will of the people is the will of Heaven;
No one can resist it!

Who is made afraid by threat?
Who is made afraid by violence?

Better to die fighting,
Than to die of gnawing hunger.

Students, rise! Workers, struggle!
Farmers, join the fray!

Shake the heavens and the earth;
The spirits of our brothers will protect you.

Who can stop us? Who can slow us?
Who will block the way?

Anguished policemen sympathize;
Soldiers denounce the regime!

Absolute power corrupts absolutely;
Absolute power shall be totally destroyed!

Rise up together, stand up together,
Overthrowing the brutal rule!

In April Revolution's spirit,
Struggle on for democratic rights!

Let nothing keep us from our freedom!
Let tyranny no longer reign!

Arise, spirit of self-determination!
Guide our destiny!

And we will sing the song of peace,
In freedom, justice, and love.

Yung Chung Ho was only twenty. But I was left with no doubts about the determination behind that voice. South

Korea and South Africa and all other oppressive regimes had better listen to the voice of the young who are saying it loud and clear, that the cry of the people will never be put down by the gun.

Notes

1. An article that appeared in *The Weekly Review* of 13 September 1976.

12 The South Korean People's Struggle

Is the Struggle of all Oppressed Peoples

▲▲

I want to thank the organizers of the Emergency International Conference on Korea. I know very little about the Korean people's struggle for national unity and democracy. Of course I do know that they were among the first Asian people to strike a mortal blow at American imperialism. I also know that they have a country which is partitioned, with one half under U.S. imperialism and that the other half has been liberated and is a people's Korea. But that is about all I know. I come from a country whose press is owned by foreigners and which always sides with imperialism. Thus it tells us little about the happenings and struggles in the oppressed countries. When it reports on such events it does so with the view of obscuring the truth or showing that imperialist domination is a good thing and that anti-imperialist struggles are bad. Thus I have come here to learn. I want to carry home something about the Korean people's just struggle for national liberation. I would like to make it clear that I'm not speaking for any organization in Kenya or Korea and that for the purposes of this meeting I am non-aligned: but then we were told that this conference was for non-aligned persons and was paralleling the Non-Aligned Nations Conference in Colombo! I am here in my capacity as a writer who tries to speak about myself and who tries to get his inspiration from the struggles of our people for total liberation from imperialism and any form of foreign domination. That means that as a writer I can never be non-aligned. How can a writer, if he is to be meaningful, assume a non-aligned position amid a million voices crying out in unison for the right to control the natural and human resources of their own land; the right to control the fruits of their sweat, the products of their labour? How can one be non-aligned in the very sight of a million muscles flexing to

break centuries of chains tied around their bodies by imperialism and all the exploiting classes?

Yesterday I was moved to tears by the testimony of the
Korean composer Yun I Sang, when he described his experiences in the cages of Park Chung Hee. I was impressed with his
statement that he gained strength to compose opera in prison
from the knowledge that he was speaking for many gagged
voices, for the many whose bodies were being tortured. That's
an example of the position that music and the arts in the
oppressed must take. Speak for, speak to, speak out for the
strength and determination of the people in their struggle for
total liberation.

It is the position taken by Kim Chi Ha in his poetry. That is
why his poems speak not only to Koreans but to all the struggling peoples in the world. He is in prison but his voice is an
inspiration to us in South Africa and Zimbabwe, to us in Palestine, to us in all countries under neo-colonialism. When he
speaks of the Five Bandits which, in alliance with U.S. imperialism, are helping in the plunder and murder of our peoples, he
is speaking about all our histories.

Let me dwell for a few minutes on that history which we all
share. It has two dialectically related aspects. First, it has been
a history of exploitation and oppression by the western European ruling classes. We may remember that Portuguese mercenary
explorers and sailors landed in Africa at the close of the fifteenth
century on a mission to find the shortest sea-route to the wealth
of Asia. The ruling feudal classes and the emergent mercantile
bourgeoisie both wanted this route to theft and plunder. They
wanted gold, glittering gold! In pursuit of this glittering yellow
metal and shining white ivory they wantonly destroyed many
advanced cities, especially those along the East African coast.
They destroyed cities in Mozambique, Zanzibar, and in Kenya.
It was these Portuguese hunters for gold and ivory who destroyed
Zimbabwe, a city of stone and well-laid streets, and turned
them into ruins. They had gunpowder on their side and, of
course, the Holy Bible. It is interesting that at the time they
were planting missionaries in Korea and other parts of Asia,
they were doing the same in Africa. Their wanton destruction
of human lives was part and parcel of their destruction of cities
and cultures. Remember what they wanted was gold, silver,
ivory and spices, anything that would bring instant profit to the

feudal and bourgeois classes in Portugal. Their new bourgeois splendour was based on the corpses and blood of murdered Africans. Their so-called civilization was built on the destruction of highly advanced African civilizations. Fort Jesus in Mombasa, Kenya, built by the predators from Portugal, still stands as an ugly monument to their short-lived glory and success as a major European colonialist power. They were only an advance party of other European powers with equally nothing more than the possession of gunpowder to boast about. But the gunpowder worked. . . . Africans died, their cattle died, their houses fell, the great migrations and movements inland started. They would try to build new houses, new cities and new lives, but even this was not to be. More hordes of European colonialist predators came from the sea.

The history of European exploitation, domination and oppression of African nations and peoples falls into three main phases:

(1) *Slavery*: This was the period when Africans were seized as slaves and were shipped across the seas to build the New World of America, the West Indies and Latin America. When you contemplate western industrial and technological growth — later transported to Japan — remember that it too was built on the enslaved labour of Africans. On the other side, you can see the terrible negative consequences of this transplanting of labour on Africa's own growth. Human beings are the subject and object of any development, for it is their combined labour power that changes nature and hence changes themselves. You cannot kill people, you cannot cage people, you cannot scatter people, making them beggars in their own land or in other lands and still call it development.

(2) *Classical colonialism*: Then came the period of direct colonial occupation. This was characterized by the exploitation of Africa's natural resources and the exploitation of African labour by European capital. Africa became the source of raw materials, the source of cheap labour and also a market for European goods. This exploitation was accompanied by direct political rule and direct oppression and suppression of the people by colonial armies and police.

(3) *Neo-colonialism*: Then came the period of neo-colonialism under which most of Africa now lives. This has also been called the stage or the period of 'flag independence'. This means a

situation where a client indigenous government is ruling and oppressing people on behalf of American, European and Japanese capital. Such a regime acts as a policeman of international capital and often mortgages a whole country for arms and crumbs from the masters' table. It never changes the colonial economy of development and uneven development.

All these three stages are accompanied by brutality and oppression — in fact, all these three stages are nothing but different aspects of slavery. Just now as we are talking in this hall, African workers' children are being killed in South Africa. Just now as we are talking so many of our people are being tortured in South Africa and Zimbabwe — not to mention many others being killed or rotting in jails in many neo-colonial states in Africa, including Uganda and Kenya. But what I have been talking about is only one aspect of the history which we share with Korea and many other Asian countries.

The other and more enduring aspect is that of struggle and resistance. The several hundred years of European slavery in Africa has given rise to an infinitely glorious and heroic history of the people who have refused to succumb to exploitation and oppression. African people fought the British, Portuguese, French and other European slave-drivers. They fought and struggled against the colonial armies of occupation. There are many glorious sagas of this period. I may cite the Algerian armed struggle against the French, and the Kenyan Mau Mau armed resistance against the British. You may be interested to know that the Mau Mau liberation struggle in Kenya was being waged at about the same time as the Korean War. More recently, there have been the successful armed struggles in Mozambique, Angola and Guinea Bissau. Armed struggle is still going on in Zimbabwe. We can see the beginnings of a similar armed struggle in South Africa: Soweto is only a beginning of things to come. I believe that the recent victories of the people in Angola, Mozambique and Guinea Bissau have ushered in a new era in the struggles of the African peoples. Just as the Portuguese were the first to introduce the era of slavery and colonialism in the fifteenth century, so their forced departure signifies the end of classical colonialism in Africa and the beginning of strenuous struggles against imperialism in the neo-colonial stage. Neo-colonialism thrives because of the alliance between a native *comprador* class and a foreign bourgeoisie. The *comprador* class rules by torture, fraud, imprisonment, military brutality, terror and so on to suppress the people on behalf of their paymasters in London, Paris, New York, Amsterdam and Tokyo. They are, if you like, the present day slave-drivers and plantation overseers hired by international monopoly capital.

The native comprador class is the most dangerous because it confuses the people. The real masters are invisible. The visible apparent rulers seem to wear the same skin and certainly seem to speak the same tongue as the rest of the people. But they kill democracy and they kill national initiative. They kill unity under the pretence of fighting communism.

But the struggle will continue simultaneously against this *comprador* native ruling class and against the foreign international aggressors, as well as against the Park Chung Hees of the oppressed world and their foreign paymasters. That's why the Korean people's struggle for democracy and unity is the struggle of all oppressed people.

I believe that peace is only possible through the total burial of imperialism. So our struggle for national unity and democracy necessarily is a struggle against imperialism and foreign domination. But the imperialist powers are co-operating and sharing information and strategies, so all the oppressed and exploited peoples must also unite to smash and bury the enemy for ever.

The enemy is now led by U.S. imperialism. After the U.S. defeat in Vietnam and Cambodia, the imperialists have retreated and are now attempting to consolidate their positions in Africa, the Middle East, Latin America, Korea and other South-East Asian countries. You remember that after Vietnam, the U.S. Defence Secretary threatened to use nuclear weapons against the Korean people should they continue to refuse to be slaves in their own land. More recently, the U.S. Defence Secretary visited Kenya and Zaïre to conclude secret defence agreements. Kissinger has been meeting the South African Hitlerite, Vorster, in West Germany to hatch out more plots to continue mounting armed attacks in Africa just as previously the same Hitlerite Vorster met with his Zionist collaborators in Israel. And France has been selling new nuclear plants to the Hitlerite Vorster. The threat of nuclear war thus obviously still comes from the mad dog, rampaging imperialist countries.

Thus it is more than obvious why we in Asia, Africa and

Latin America must support the Korean people's struggle for national unity and democracy. We must not see our struggle in isolation. South Africa, Zimbabwe, Palestine, Chile, Korea — it's all the same battle against the enemy of democracy and the unity of peoples; we must therefore consciously forge unity of all the oppressed world peoples. I said that I was not speaking for an organization. But I am sure that the Kenyan people who have consistently stood against the position of a division of their own country and who have stood firmly against any foreign claims on their territory, will firmly support the Korean people's just demand for national reunification and for democracy.

Long live the Korean people's struggle! Long live the struggle of all the peasants and workers in the world! Long live the unity of all peoples in the world struggling against imperialism and all forms of foreign domination!!

Notes

1. Speech read during the International Emergency Conference on Korea held in Tokyo, 12—14 August 1976.

13 The Robber and the Robbed

Two Antagonistic Images in Afro-American
Literature and Thought[1]

▲▲

I was asked to speak on 'Literature and the Evolution of Black
Consciousness: The Making of an Image'. But there is not one
image: there is not one black consciousness in Afro-American
literature. There are in fact two opposing consciousnesses, two
images, two opposing trends in Afro-American literature and
thought shaped by the different persons' perception of the
nature of American society. Now the images we have for ourselves in relationship to other selves, or the images we have of
other people in relationship to ourselves are dependent on the
place we occupy in the system of production, ownership and
hence our power over the share-out of the national wealth.
It matters whether we are only part of the productive forces,
suppliers and sellers of the labour power which alone, with
instruments of labour acting on nature, produces wealth; or
whether we are merely the owners of the means of production
hiring the labour powers of others: Whether in other words we
are the *robbed* or the *robbers*.

The minority who reap where they never planted, who pocket
the wealth produced by the working-labouring-majority, are
able to rob with impunity even, because in the evolution of that
society they have come to control the state with all its coercive,
violent powers, and to control the other social institutions with
all their hidden powers of psychological coercion and mental
conditioning. Thus their historical task of robbing the majority
is made easier both by their seizure of the state and its mani-
fold powers, and by their control of the instruments of subtle
persuasion, of the cultural tools that forge certain images, that
develop a given consciousness. If the robbers of wealth are able
to instil images of defeat, unsureness, division, inferiority complex, helplessness, fawning, abject humility, slavishness in the

minds of the robbed, then they can eat their loot in comfort
and sleep in peace. Thus, it has always been in the interests of
a robbing minority to control the minds, the consciousness of
the working majority — the true producers of wealth — by all
the educational, literary, communicational, cultural and aesthetic means at their disposal.

But the robbed do not always acquiesce. They have always
struggled for the control of the wealth they have produced. To
do so, they have found it imperative to, at the same time,
struggle against all the oppressive social institutions erected on
the structure of theft and robbery. In the process of so struggling, they evolve images embodying a consciousness corresponding to the objective needs and demands of their struggle, a
consciousness that is directly and diametrically opposed to that
of the exploiting and hence oppressing minority. There are thus
two warring ideologies in a society built on a system of robbery
and theft corresponding to the two antagonistic positions of the
robber and the robbed, of the parasitic and the creative, in the
social production of wealth.

The two consciousnesses are necessarily at war with one
another because they are reflections of the actual warring political and economic positions of the two classes in society. The
two consciousnesses do not remain static: they change even as
the productive forces in society change and hence as the relations of production (the relations of the robber class and the
robbed class) change in time.

The battlefield of the two consciousnesses is the working
majority. The ruling robbing class and idle minority want the
working people to perceive themselves in a negative manner.
They want the robbed to look at the world through the eyes of
the robber. But the conditions of their existence and the objective demands of their position call, in the robbed, for a
different kind of consciousness, a different way of looking at
the world. For the robbing minority, reality is final, is static,
is given, is divinely willed, it cannot change. For the robbed, the
present conditions, the present reality, cannot be final, absolute,
unchanging. The world must change, must be changed.

Spokesmen of the robbed and the oppressed (or those pur-
porting to speak for the oppressed, or those recruited from the
oppressed) oscillate between the ideology, the consciousness,
that bespeaks the objective needs of the exploiting minority

(i.e. we have the best of all possible worlds; that there has been and always will be the robber and the robbed; human nature will never change, human nature is selfish; we only need minor reforms, a few adjustments within this best of all possible worlds; etc.) and that ideology, that consciousness, which represents the needs of the struggling majority (i.e. the rejection of eternal, unchanging human nature; the recognition and affirmation of change as a constant theme in nature and society; the affirmation of the necessity not only to explain the world but also to change it; that the masses are the most revolutionary part of society's productive forces; etc.).

All this can best be seen if we look at the relationship between Afro-Americans and Euro-Americans over the last two hundred years. The ruling robbing minority has always been Euro-American. The Afro-American has, by and large, been part of the robbed working majority. But the Afro-American worker has been the most exploited, the most oppressed section of the working majority. Racism and racist theories have been effectively used by the ruling Euro-American minority of robbers and thieves to divide the robbed majority — Afro-American, Euro-American, Asio-American — by bribing the Euro-American working class with titbits of the loot cruelly robbed from the Afro-American workers, and also by feeding the Euro-American worker with spurious fascist notions of racial superiority, and the Afro-American worker with equally spurious notions of racial inferiority.

Thus, the Afro-American masses have been the greatest victims of two hundred years of the growth of American capitalism to its current position of leader of world imperialism; two hundred years of economic exploitation; four hundred years of repressive socio-political institutions; two centuries of a racist ruling class ideology and consciousness. By the same token, the Afro-American workers have been at the forefront of economic struggles, of political struggles, and thus, at the forefront in the evolution of a consciousness containing all the gems of the most advanced ideas and objectives of total liberation. This is true whether one is talking about the American Declaration of Independence (all the notions in that Declaration were first articulated in the slave revolts and songs); or about the consciousness animating the Republican side in the American Civil War (again, Lincoln's statements were forestalled in the

slave escapes to the North, the continuing slave revolts and
declarations, and in the slave narratives); or about the struggle
of the American people against occupation of Vietnam. Therefore, the two consciousnesses, the two warring and opposed
images, the two world outlooks of the robber and the robbed,
can best be illustrated in Afro-American literature and thought.

Afro-American writers and spokesmen range from those who
hold positions that correspond to those of the ruling Euro-
American class of robbers, to those who hold positions and
articulate a consciousness that corresponds to that of the foremost and most advanced forces of change in American society.
These two trends in Afro-American literature and thought are
easily seen in their image of Africa; in their attitudes to the
class struggle in America; in their attitudes to American capitalism and imperialism. For the purpose of this talk I shall not
draw on the people's oral literature because here the ideas of
total liberation from bondage, the acceptance of self and of
one's origins, the feeling that the social institutions of capitalism are exploitative and rotten, the ideas of violent struggle
to change society, have been consistent and have been en-
shrined in the slave songs and folk poetry. Here, in the popular
people's tradition, there is no compromise with the ideology
and consciousness of the ruling class. I shall illustrate my thesis
by drawing on the literature by that army of spokesmen that
can either choose to articulate the correct position of the people;
or to obscure, confuse, in order to aid the enemy of the people.

As early as 1773, Phyllis Wheatley had swallowed whole the
images of Africa contained in the works of European writers,
such as Hume and other spokesmen for slavery and the slave
trade, so that for her Africa was 'the land of errors, and Egyptian
gloom'. She was all gratitude for having been rescued in safety
from 'those dark abodes'.

> Twas mercy brought me from my Pagan land,
> Taught my benighted soul to understand
> That there's a God, that there's a Saviour too.
> Once I redemption neither sought nor knew.
> Some view our sable race with scornful eyes;
> 'Their colour is a diabolic dye.'
> Remember, Christians, Negroes, black as Cain.
> May be refined, and join the angelic train.[2]

This was not any different from the position of Thomas Jefferson, the Secretary of State under Washington, (to the latter Wheatley had written an enthusiastic poem and a letter saying how his appointment as a general of the North American armies had excited sensations not easy to suppress) who wrote in 1785:

I advance it, therefore, as a suspicion only, that the blacks, whether originally a distinct race, or made distinct by time and circumstances, are inferior to the whites in the endowments both of body and mind. . . . This unfortunate difference of colour, and perhaps of faculty, is a powerful obstacle to the emancipation of these people.[3]

Yet Africans were the main productive force of the American economy: Phyllis Wheatley's position corresponds to the consciousness of the then ruling, slave-holding classes that rationalized degradation of the masses on the basis of racist theories of the African continent and the African past.

But, even during this era of slavery and slave trade, there were those who refused to espouse the slave mentality and ruling class ideologies and instead articulated a consciousness of emancipation and liberation.

Olaudah Equiano, like Wheatly, had been abducted from Africa in his youth and so retained memories of his past. In his book, *The Interesting Narrative of the Life of Olaudah Equiano, or Gustavus Vassa, the African*, he wrote of his Africa in terms of a nation of dancers, musicians and poets. He talked of the plain manner of his people's living. He wrote positively of their manufactures of golden ornaments, of their spinning and weaving of cotton, and of other manufactures like earthen vessels. He was again positive about their architecture in which 'we study convenience rather than ornament'. He was even more profuse in his memories of the abundance of the land:

Our land is uncommonly rich and fruitful, and produces all kinds of vegetables in great abundance. We have plenty of Indian corn, and vast quantities of cotton and tobacco. Our pineapples grow without culture; they are about the size of the largest sugar-loaf and finely flavoured. We have also spices of different kinds, particularly pepper, and a variety of delicious fruits which I have never seen in Europe,

together with gums of various kinds and honey in abundance. All our industry is exerted to improve those blessings
of nature. Agriculture is our chief employment, and everyone, even the children and women, are engaged in it. Thus
we are all habituated to labour from our earliest years.
Everyone contributes something to the common stock,
and as we are unacquainted with idleness we have no
beggars.[4]

In the same tradition, Benjamin Banneker, a self-trained and
self-taught African genius of physics, mathematics and astro-
nomy could in 1792 reply to Thomas Jefferson in bold words
of courage and great social awareness:

I freely and cheerfully acknowledge, that I am of the
African race, and in that colour which is natural to them,
of the deepest dye; and it is under a sense of the most profound gratitude to the Supreme Ruler of the Universe, that
I now confess to you, that I am not under that state of
tyrannical thraldom, and inhuman captivity, to which many
of my brethren are doomed, but that I have abundantly
tasted of the fruition of those blessings, which proceed
from that free and unequalled liberty with which you are
favoured; and which I hope you will willingly allow you
have mercifully received, from the immediate hand of that
being from whom proceedeth every good and perfect gift.
    Suffer me to recall to your mind that time, in which the
arms of the British crown were exerted, with every powerful effort, in order to reduce you to a state of servitude:
Look back, I entreat you, on the variety of dangers to
which you were exposed; reflect on that period in which
every human aid appeared unavailable, and in which even
hope and fortitude wore the aspect of inability to the conflict, and you cannot but be led to a serious and grateful
sense of your miraculous and providential preservation;
you cannot but acknowledge, that the present freedom
and tranquillity which you enjoy, you have mercifully
received, and that it is the peculiar blessing of heaven.
    This, Sir, was a time when you clearly saw into the
injustice of a state of Slavery, and in which you had just
apprehension of the horrors of its condition. It was then

that your abhorence thereof was so excited, that you publicly held forth this true and invaluable doctrine, which is worthy to be recorded and remembered in all succeeding ages: 'We hold these truths to be self-evident, that all men are created equal; that they are endowed by their Creator with certain inalienable rights, and that among these are life, liberty, and the pursuit of happiness.'

Here was a time in which your tender feelings for ourselves had engaged you thus to declare; you were then impressed with proper ideas of the great violation of liberty, and the free possession of those blessings, to which you were entitled by nature; but, sire, *how pitiable it is to reflect, that although you were so fully convinced of the benevolence of the Father of Mankind and of his equal and impartial distribution of these rights and privileges which he hath conferred upon them, that you should at the same time counteract his mercies, in detaining by fraud and violence, so numerous a part of my brethren under groaning captivity and cruel oppression, that you should at the same time be found guilty of that most criminal act, which you professedly detested in others, with respect to yourselves.*[5] (Italics mine)

Banneker's tradition was continued in one of the finest minds and one of the most courageous fighters of the nineteenth century. Frederick Douglass was another self-taught genius, who rose from a state in which he was 'so pinched with hunger as to dispute with Old "Nep", the dog, for the crumbs which fell from the kitchen table'; to a leading position in the struggle for the emancipation of Afro-Americans and other oppressed, enslaved Americans. As he said:

. . . Though I am more closely connected and identified with one class of outrage, oppressed and enslaved people, I cannot allow myself to be insensible to the wrongs and suffering of any part of the great family of man. I am not only an American slave, but a man, and as such, am bound to use my powers for the welfare of the whole human brotherhood. . . . I believe that the sooner the wrongs of the whole human family are made known, the sooner those wrongs will be reached.[6]

His autobiography, *Life and Times of Frederick Douglass*
should be a must in all our schools and colleges both because of
its tremendous strengths and for Douglass's failures toward the
end of his life when he was lured into serving American imperialism in Haiti. But the early part of his life and his speeches
clearly show the only path open to people and classes who want
to be free. He was not squeamish about revolutionary violence,
even on the personal level. He relates how when he became a
slave of Thomas Auld, he was handed to an Edward Covey, a
slave-breaker. He describes the beatings, the overwork, the
degradation in what he calls the period he was made to drink
the bitterest cup of slavery, until he decided to stand up to
Covey and fight him:

> This battle with Mr Covey, undignified as it was and as I
> fear my narration of it is, was the turning point in my 'life
> as a slave'. It rekindled in my breast the smouldering
> embers of liberty. It brought up my Baltimore dreams and
> revived a sense of my own manhood. I was a changed being
> after that fight. I was nothing before — I was a man now.
> It recalled to life my crushed self-respect, and my self-
> confidence, and inspired me with a renewed determination
> to be a free man. A man without force is without the
> essential dignity of humanity. Human nature is so con-
> stituted, that it cannot honour a helpless man, though it
> can pity him, and even this it cannot do long if signs of
> power do not arise. . . .
> I was no longer a servile coward, trembling under the
> frown of a brother worm of the dust, but my long-cowed
> spirit was roused to an attitude of independence. I had
> reached the point at which I was *not afraid to die*. This
> spirit made me a freeman in fact, though I still remained
> a slave in *form*. When a slave cannot be flogged, he is more
> than half free. He has a domain as broad as his own manly
> heart to defend, and he is really 'a power on earth'.[7]

He never forgot the violent combat and his own personal
struggle to escape from slavery. In his speeches he always insisted on the primacy of the struggle of the oppressed classes
and peoples. He was later to argue that without struggle there
could never be progress:

The whole history of the progress of human liberty shows that all concessions, yet made to her august claims, have been born of earnest struggle. The conflict has been exciting, agitating, all-absorbing, and for the time being putting all other tumults to silence. It must do this or it does nothing. If there is no struggle, there is no progress. Those who profess to favour freedom, and yet depreciate agitation, are men who want crops without plowing up the ground. They want rain without thunder and lightning. They want the ocean without the awful roar of its many waters. This struggle may be a moral one; or it may be a physical one; or it may be both moral and physical; but it must be a struggle. *Power concedes nothing without demand. It never did, and it never will. Find out just what people will submit to, and you have found out the exact amount of injustice and wrong which will be imposed upon them; and these will continue till they are resisted with either words or blows, or with both. The limits of tyrants are prescribed by the endurance of those whom they oppress.* In light of these ideas, Negroes [sic] will be hunted at the North and held and flogged at the South, so long as they submit to these devilish outrages, and make no resistance, either moral or physical. Men may not get all they pay for in this world; but they must certainly pay for all they get. If we ever get free from all the oppression and wrongs heaped upon us, we must pay for their removal. We must do this by labour, by suffering, by sacrifice, and if needs be, by our lives, and the lives of others.[8] (italics mine)

You can see that he is espousing a different kind of consciousness from that of Wheatley or that of Booker T. Washington. Washington continues the tradition of Wheatley but even more slavishly. He articulated better than most members of the Euro-American ruling class the racist ideology that rationalized the oppression of Afro-American workers. His autobiography, *Up From Slavery* could better have been entitled: *Back To Slavery*:

. . . When we rid ourselves of prejudices, or racial feeling, and look facts in the face, we must acknowledge that,

notwithstanding the cruelty and moral wrong of slavery,
the ten million Negroes [sic] inhabiting this country, who
themselves or whose ancestors went through the school of
American slavery, are in a stronger and more hopeful condition, materially, intellectually, morally, and religiously,
than is true of an equal number of black people in any
other portion of the globe. This is so to such an extent
that Negroes in this country, who themselves or whose
forefathers went through the school of slavery, are con-
stantly returning to Africa as missionaries to enlighten
those who remained in the fatherland. . . .

*Ever since I have been old enough to think for myself, I
have entertained the idea that, notwithstanding the cruel
wrongs inflicted upon us, the black man got nearly as
much out of slavery as the white man did.*[9] (italics mine)

He is ecstatic about the fact that during the Civil War, some
of the slaves would even beg for the privilege of sitting up at
night to nurse the wounded masters:

This tenderness and sympathy on the part of those held in
bondage was a result of their kindly and generous nature.
In order to defend and protect the women and children
who were left on the plantation when the white males
went to war, the slaves would have laid down their lives.
The slave who was selected to sleep in the 'big house' during
the absence of the males was considered to have the place
of honour. Any one attempting to harm 'young Mistress'
or 'old Mistress' during the night would have had to cross
the dead body of the slave to do so. I do not know how
many have noticed it, but I think that it will be found to
be true that there are few instances, either in slavery or
freedom, in which a member of my race has been known
to betray a specific trust.[10]

When freedom came, he writes, the slaves were almost as well
fitted to begin life anew as the master, except in the matters of
book learning and ownership of property. And yet a few pages
later he is almost ecstatic about the inability of 'negroes' to
cope with the life of freedom and hence the stealthy return of
some to the slave condition:

The wild rejoicing on the part of the emancipated coloured people lasted but for a brief period, for I noticed that by the time they returned to their cabins there was a change in their feelings. The great responsibility of being free, of having charge of themselves, of having to think and plan for themselves and their children, seemed to take possession of them. It was very much like suddenly turning a youth of ten or twelve years out into the world to provide for himself. In a few hours the great questions with which the Anglo-Saxon race had been grappling for centuries had been thrown upon these people to be solved. These were the questions of a home, a living, the rearing of children, education, citizenship, and the establishment and support of churches. Was it any wonder that within a few hours the wild rejoicing ceased and a feeling of deep gloom seemed to pervade the slave quarter? To some it seemed that, now that they were in actual possession of it, freedom was a more serious thing than they had expected to find it. Some of the slaves were seventy or eighty years old: their best days were gone. They had no strength with which to earn a living in a strange place and among strange people, even if they had been sure where to find a new place of abode. To this class the problem seemed especially hard. Besides, deep down in their hearts there was a strange and peculiar attachment to 'old Marster' and 'old Missus', and to their children, which they found it hard to think of breaking off. With these they had spent in some cases nearly a half-century, and it was no light thing to think of parting. Gradually, one by one, stealthily at first, the older slaves began to wander from the slave quarters back to the 'big house' to have a whispered conversation with their former owners as to the future.[11]

Up From Slavery is really a song in praise of social and mental subjugation, fawning, self-humiliation and self-abjection. It is a hymn in praise of the consciousness, the world-view of the master, the slave-driver, the colonizer, the imperialist, the oppressor. It calls upon the oppressed, the robbed, to accept the condition of their robbery and oppression with gleeful gratitude. It goes further and blames them for their slavery. This is clearer in his so-called 'Atlanta Exposition Address':

The wisest among my race understand that the agitation of questions of social equality is the extremest folly, and that progress in the enjoyment of all the privileges that will come to us must be the result of severe and constant struggle rather than of artificial forcing. No race that has anything to contribute to the markets of the world is long in any degree ostracized. It is important and right that all privileges of the law be ours, but it is vastly more important that we be prepared for the exercises of these privileges. The opportunity to earn a dollar in a factory just now is worth infinitely more than the opportunity to spend a dollar in an opera house.[12]

The neo-slave who rejoices at his slavery is a most pathetic creature indeed. Booker T. Washington wept tears of gratitude when, after urging his people to start at the bottom where they had always been anyway, 'Governor Bullock rushed across the platform and took me by the hand and others (the whites) did the same'.

The two consciousnesses represented by Douglass and Washington have continued to plague Afro-American literature and thought. The sell-out position of Wheatley and Washington has been continued in writers like Martin Luther King, James Baldwin, Ralph Ellison, Whitney Young, Eldridge Cleaver and other thinkers and spokesmen who have allied themselves with the consciousness of the exploiting and oppressing minority (i.e. do not struggle violently; we can reform the system of capitalism and make it work). The other trend of Banneker/ David Walker-Douglass (the early Douglass) has been continued in the work of people like Du Bois, Paul Robeson, Richard Wright, Malcolm X and George Jackson. Most others tend to oscillate between the two positions. Even within the work and life of the same writer one may get this oscillation between espousing an oppressor-class consciousness and espousing the consciousness of the exploited and oppressed.

Malcolm X forms a very important departure in Afro-American thought. Through involvement in the struggle, he came to see that the root cause of Afro-American oppression lay, not in the sinfulness and biological depravity of whiteness, but in the very system of social production of wealth, in the very system of ownership of the wealth produced by the majority. Capitalism was a system of the robber and the robbed. Except that the Afro-American worker has been not only the object of economic robbery but also of cultural and racist oppression. Capitalism was then at the root of the slave consciousness. To fight for total liberation then, one had to see the social basis of exploitation and oppression; capitalism and the class that maintained it had to go. This led Malcolm X to see the nature of American imperialism. Hence, he would now tell the Afro-American workers that the forces oppressing a child in the Congo, in South Africa, were the same as those doing the same to a child in Mississippi. Thus, within a very short time he had travelled the road that Du Bois had travelled all his life.

The Du Bois/Malcolm X line is being continued by writers like Imamu Baraka who has now abandoned his earlier mystical and limiting standpoint of cultural nationalism. He has come to recognize the class basis of Afro-American oppression; that American capitalism at home and American imperialism in Africa are at the root of that continued robbery and theft of the social product created by the combined power of the Afro-American working class and other workers from other racial nationalities in America. His address to the Sixth Pan-African Congress is important in this respect because it shows a definite movement towards an unequivocal articulation of an anti-imperialist consciousness, a definite stand against the American ruling class robbery not only of the wealth of American people but that of all other peoples, especially in Africa:

The conscious determination to struggle demands the conscious creation of systems of struggle. The Tanzania recruitment programme of Africans in the diaspora represents a small initiating step in creating some aspect of a revolutionary Pan-African culture. With the same seriousness with which NATO or SEATO or EEC, or GATT were created, as examples of imperialist 'integration' (to cut down rivalry between imperialists and jointly exploit the rest of the world), so the anti-imperialist forces throughout the world must have a similar integration. And Africans, oppressed and struggling in various parts of the world, must be integrated into a truly Pan-African anti-imperialist system. One that utilizes the democratic and socialist element of each society, the revolutionary, anti-bourgeois quality of each of these African communities, the national cultures linked together as *an international anti-imperialist culture*. We can only build an actual Pan-African culture by defeating petty-bourgeois statism and neo-colonialism and the rule of imperialist borders and treaties. Only by creating systems and institutions based on revolutionary ideology, incorporating Revolutionary Nationalism, Pan-Africanism and truly scientific Socialism. Which means socialism based on analysis of our own social structures, through utilizing the universally applicable scientific method, and international revolutionary experiences.[13]

Should this be reflected in his creative imaginative work, it will mark a definite landmark in the evolution of a people's consciousness in Afro-American literature and thought.

We who are gathered at Abidjan cannot escape from the two consciousnesses I have tried to outline. We can choose to continue the line of Wheatley/Washington/Whitney Young and become the black spokesmen of American imperialism in our own continent, or we can put ourselves at the service of the struggle of African people — the peasants, and the workers — against imperialism at all the levels: economic, political, and ideological. We can thus continue and strengthen the line of Banneker/Douglass/Du Bois/Jackson/Malcolm X/ Baraka (his latter self) and forge a consciousness that never compromises with the path of sell-out to imperialism and to all the classes that benefit from exploitation and oppression of peoples.

In this, we may want to remember what American imperialism, its social institutions and its ideological weapons mean to us who only the other day saw Kissinger come to make a deal with South Africa. We may borrow words from Frederick Douglass who once posed the question of the meaning of the fourth of July:

> What, to the American slave, is your fourth of July? I answer: A day that reveals to him, more than all other days in the year, the gross injustice and cruelty to which he is the constant victim. To him, your celebration is a sham, your boasted liberty, an unholy licence; your national

greatness, swelling vanity; your sounds of rejoicing are empty and heartless; your denunciation of tyrants, brass fronted impudence; your shouts of liberty and equality, hollow mockery; your prayers and hymns, your sermons and thanksgivings, with all your religious parade and solemnity, are to him, mere bombast, fraud, deception, impiety, and hypocrisy — a thin veil to cover up crimes which would disgrace a nation of savages. There is not a nation on the earth guilty of practices more shocking and bloody than are the people of the United States, at this very hour.

Go where you may, search where you will, roam through all the monarchies and despotisms of the Old World, travel through South America, search out every abuse, and when you have found the last, lay your facts by the side of the everyday practices of this nation, and you will say with me, that, *for revolting barbarity and shameless hypocrisy, America reigns without a rival.*[14] (italics mine)

I believe that these words are as true today as they were when they were spoken in 1842. American imperialism having been defeated in South-East Asia is trying to consolidate in Africa. But the African people have given the answer. They will no longer continue to build America and western Europe, from the days of mercantile capitalism, through slavery and the slave trade, through *laissez-faire* capitalism to the present era of imperialism in the last stage of neo-colonialism. We shall no longer continue to cultivate and plant for others, the imperialist bourgeoisie and their overseer *comprador* class, to reap.

The African proletariat and the peasantry and the working people of Asia and Latin America are telling it to U.S. imperialist bourgeoisie: We will not let you and your local *Nyapara* allies reap where you never planted.

That for me seems to be the significant change of attitude to American imperialism in this bi-centennial year of the foundation of the United States of America; the rejection of the robber consciousness and attitudes, and their replacement by the revolutionary consciousness of the robbed of the world as expressed in their literature, life and thought. It is a position once articulated by the poet of democracy, Walt Whitman, when he wrote:

Those corpses of young men,
Those martyrs that hang from gibbets —
  those hearts pierced by grey lead,
Cold and motionless as they seem, live
  elsewhere with unslaughtered vitality.

They live in other young men, O kings!
They live in brothers, again ready to defy you![15]

Notes

1. Paper presented to the American Studies Regional Conference, Abidjan, 26—8 July, 1976.
2. G. Herbert Renfro, Life and Works of Phillis Wheatley, 1916, p. 48.

Index

▲▲